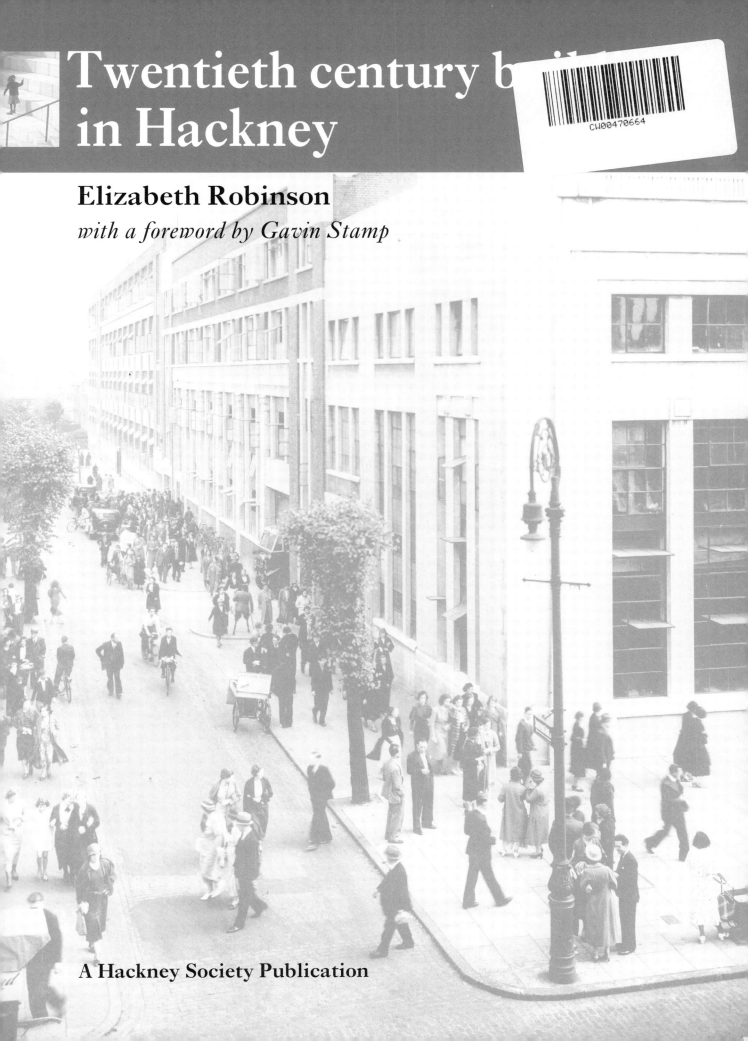

Twentieth century buildings in Hackney

Elizabeth Robinson
with a foreword by Gavin Stamp

A Hackney Society Publication

RENAISI

The Hackney Society gratefully acknowledges financial support received from Hackney Parochial Charities, English Heritage and Renaisi which has helped to fund this publication.

Published by The Hackney Society, The Round Chapel, 1d Glenarm Road, London E5 0LY telephone 020 8985 6760

ISBN 0 9536734 0 5

Typeset in Ehrhardt (issued by Monotype, 1937)
Designed by Sue Clarke
for Expression Printers Ltd, IP23 8HH

The Hackney Society was founded in 1969 to encourage the improvement of the environment of the London Borough of Hackney, its buildings, streets and parks. As a pressure group of local residents, the Society is dependent on the help of volunteers, and the more people participate in its activities, the more effective it can be.

The Society meets monthly for a programme of walks and talks about the history and built environment of the Borough, and has published books and walks on that subject which are available from bookshops and local libraries.

For further information about the Society or its publications, please contact us at the address above.

front cover The Simpson Factory.
View taken from Stoke Newington Road
looking down Somerford Grove, 1935

Contents

In loving memory of Michael Stratton,
admirer of 20th century buildings in Hackney and elsewhere

Acknowledgements

The idea for this book began with a very stimulating Thirties Society (now the Twentieth Century Society) walk around central Hackney in 1992. Karen Smith, a former Hackney Society researcher, developed the idea further.

Two people in particular have helped most generously with this project, and I would like to thank them especially. Philip Ward-Jackson of the Courtauld Institute has taken many of the new photographs in the book. My husband Robert Thorne has patiently endured many questions, offered suggestions, cycled round almost every back street in Hackney with me, and read the text, making many rough places smooth. I am extremely grateful.

Many other people have helped with information about particular buildings, photographs, drawings, fund-raising, and so on. My thanks to: Derek Baker, Richard Blackwell, Bob Brown, Geremy Butler, Sheila Butterly, Bridget Cherry, Stephen Coley, Dominic Cullinan, Julia Elton, Rev. Alan Everett, David French, Madeleine Ginsburg, Bill Hall, Patrick Hammill, Ivan Harbour, Elain Harwood, John Hayward, Matthew Holden, Rev. William Hurdman, Clifford Lawton, Wayne Lindsey, Paul Maas, Frank Newby, Alan Powers, Sunand Prasad, Joanna Roberts, Andrew Saint, Michael Stratton, Marjorie Thorne, Andrew Thorp, Sarah Vaughan-Roberts, Isobel Watson, Paul Westbrook, Jack Youngmark.

Thanks are also due to the staff of many libraries and archives including: David Mander and the staff of Hackney Archives, London Metropolitan Archives, the Courtauld Institute, RIBA Library, National Monuments Record, Public Record Office.

Elizabeth Robinson
Stoke Newington, August 1999

Foreword

As a (former) South Londoner, I did not know Hackney as well as I ought to have done. Not that I was deterred by the eponymous borough's dreadful reputation, any more than by a psychological resistance to travelling north-east – my first incursions, after all, were prompted by curiosity about the (alas, now closed) viaduct that ran out of poor old Broad Street to Dalston Junction. No, the problem was pure ignorance: simply not knowing enough about the architectural riches that lie beyond Shoreditch. And it is here, in the broad field of ignorance, that the Hackney Society has been so admirably active, recognising that the conservation of fine and worthwhile buildings is very difficult without knowledge and education. Publications – like this one – are vital.

I particularly recall a pioneering booklet on the Victorian villas of Hackney, a type of study that ought to be carried out in many other parts of Britain. And now, as I am happy to applaud in this foreword, we have a rewarding investigation into the many remarkable buildings in the borough that the difficult, destructive, careless and prodigal century now drawing at last to an end has left behind. Never mind that Hackney cannot boast many ancient buildings (although there are some), for some of the most interesting urban complexes in Britain consist largely of 19th and 20th century structures.

As this book reveals, Hackney can boast a rich and diverse range of twentieth century buildings. One of my early forays was to find Charles Reilly's miniature Westminster Cathedral, that sublime vaulted space created by simple stock brick and concrete tucked away in Shacklewell. And there are other good Edwardian buildings, from Matcham's jolly, vulgar terra-cotta Empire Theatre to the young Vincent Harris's essay in simple revived Neo-Classical purity for the LCC's electric trams (but so sad that Goodhart-Rendel's Regency Revival buildings in Hackney Wick were swept away). The inter-war years left behind a fine modern Underground station by the great Holden and the seriously good German Hospital by the great Thomas Tait, of Paisley. But modernity wasn't everything, and Hackney also boasts one of the very few works in Britain by J Reginald Truelove, who did fine Classical work for the Imperial War Graves Commission in France.

As for the post war years, Hackney was naturally the scene – whether for better or worse – of many interesting experiments in public housing and public service architecture, and the representative story told in these pages comes right up to date with the work of CZWG, Penoyre & Prasad and Nigel Coates' skewed brick donut at the Geffrye Museum. There are buildings for all tastes, in fact, in underrated, long-suffering Hackney.

Gavin Stamp
Chairman of the Twentieth Century Society

Introduction

Hackney has had a bad press in recent years, but it contains some of the most interesting and vigorous 20th century architecture in London. Anyone interested in London's architecture would do well to spend a day or two exploring Hackney, and the buildings discussed in this book make a good starting point. The best buildings are spread across the length and breadth of the borough. This book concentrates on fifty examples, and this introduction sets them in context, together with some comments on what has survived and what has not.

So how different is Hackney at the end of the 20th century compared with 1900? A stroll down the Kingsland Road or Lower Clapton Road reveals a very different place compared with a hundred years ago, for Hackney is now more vibrant and culturally diverse than it has ever been. The major changes which have occurred during the 20th century are concerned with population, housing and industry.

In 1901 the population was 389,156: in 1991 it was less than half that at 181,248. Though it has a reputation of being overcrowded, the borough is in fact much less densely populated than it was a hundred years ago.

Population of Hackney during the 20th century

date	Hackney	Shoreditch	Stoke Newington*	total
1901	219,272	118,637	51,247	389,156
1911	222,533	111,390	50,659	384,582
1921	222,142	104,248	52,172	378,562
1931	215,333	97,042	51,208	363,583
1941				no census
1951	171,342	44,885	49,138	265,365
1961	164,766	40,455	52,301	257,522
1971				220,279
1981				176,676
1991				181,248

* includes area formerly known as South Hornsey

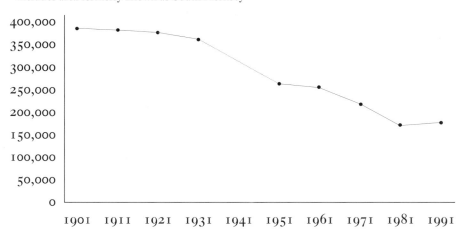

To get a sense of turn-of-the-century Hackney, the obvious source is Charles Booth's great survey, *Life and Labour of the People of London* (1902). His descriptions of many parts of the area still sound familiar: 'The general tendency during the last half century has been for Hackney to become a poorer and much more crowded quarter, but the change has not been uniform. The line of Mare Street and Clapton Road, running due North and South, divides the district into nearly equal parts, and almost all the poverty is to be found to the east of this line …' Booth described 40.2% in Shoreditch and 23.9% in Hackney and Stoke Newington as 'living in poverty'. Notably poor areas which he identified included those around the parish churches of Hackney and Homerton, to the south towards Well Street, the district immediately south of London Fields and 'the Island', a patch beside the Great Eastern Railway to the north of Hackney Downs. Of Stoke Newington he wrote, 'the district is residential rather than manufacturing. People sleep here, but work elsewhere. In Stoke Newington there are many clerks…' For present day residents, whether commuting to the City or West End, or slaving over a hot computer at home, Booth's words may still ring true.

Hackney at the end of the 20th century is still a poor place. Unemployment in March 1999 was 14.4%, one of the highest percentages in London. According to the Government *Index of Local Deprivation 1998*, the borough ranks as having the highest extent of deprivation at Ward level in England, and is ranked fourth for 'deprivation intensity' in the country (after Liverpool, Newham [east London] and Manchester). In 1998, the Department of Environment, Transport and the Regions identified Hackney as having the highest number of deprived estates in England – 112 of a national total of 1,370 such estates. Hackney has the highest percentage of population in London with no car – 61.6%. 77.1% of dwellings in Hackney are flats. So if Booth were to return to Hackney today, he would find that the basic pattern of areas of poverty and wealth has not really changed that much. What has changed is the make up of the population and the density of people across the borough.

In housing, the great revolution of this century has been the decline of the private rented sector and the development of social housing for rent, the effects of which can be seen almost everywhere in the landscape of the borough. Hackney has witnessed the immense efforts made in turn by the London County Council, Greater London Council and the boroughs to provide social housing. The first LCC schemes were Darcy and Valette Buildings (1904 and 1905), followed by the Shore Estate (1928-30) and Stamford Hill Estate (1931-39). The overall result is that the proportion of rented housing is extremely high in comparison with owner occupation. In many areas of Hackney, the levels of council housing are exceptional; in 1991 the King's Park Ward (Clapton Park, Lea Bridge etc.) had 79% council housing, Wenlock Ward (Hoxton) 78%, Haggerston Ward 77% and a further seven wards over 50%.

It is therefore not surprising that the council has to devote such a large part of its resources to dealing with its housing. A council survey of the housing stock in 1996 concluded that £500M of repairs were required to bring properties up to a basic modern standard. The amount the council may

Housing in Hackney: ownership

total dwellings in borough	75,631	%	Greater London average %
rented from local authority	36,242	47.9	
rented from housing association	8,538	11.3	
rented privately, furnished	5,631	7.4	23.3%
rented privately, unfurnished	3,735	4.9	
rented with job/business	1,127	1.5	
owner occupied, buying	16,080	21.3	57.2%
owner occupied, owned outright	4,278	5.7	

(figures from 1991 census)

borrow for such repairs is strictly controlled by government, and is currently limited to about £20M per annum. No amount of careful husbandry can really bridge a gap of this size.

Turning to industrial change, in the early decades of the century Hackney was home to many industries, primarily to service the consumer economy of the rest of London. Evidence for this survives in buildings such as the Shannon Factory built for cabinet making, and the massive Simpson Factory which employed over 3,000 people in clothing and tailoring in its heyday. Other industries typically found in the area included timber, French polishing, veneering, upholstery, boot and shoe making, printing, engraving, bookbinding, ironmongery, piano making, chemicals, colour, india rubber, jam works, and so on. The distribution of industrial activity was reflected in the character of certain areas; for example Shoreditch, with its concentration of the furniture trades, was less residential than other areas. Many people went no further than the boundaries of Hackney for their employment, not just industrial workers, but most obviously domestic servants who either lived where they worked, or very close by. Throughout the 20th century there has been a steady decline in manufacturing in the borough, and domestic service is now almost totally a thing of the past. Those who live in Hackney now work in a much wider range of places, and the borough is no longer as self-contained as it once was.

In 1900 the area was governed by two tiers of administration. At a local level, there were three boroughs, Hackney, Shoreditch and Stoke Newington, each with its own Town Hall and administrative structure. These Borough Councils came into existence in 1900 following the London Government Act of 1899, replacing the vestries, the ancient and often chronically inefficient system of local government based on parishes. The three boroughs functioned until 1965 when they were merged to constitute the present-day London Borough of Hackney. A London-wide level of government was provided by the London County Council (formed in 1889), a body which became increasingly powerful during the first half of the century. In 1965 the LCC was superseded by the Greater London Council, which operated until its abolition in 1986.

The Edwardian period was one of civic pride in institutions and great municipal building activity, partly fuelled by the advent of the new boroughs. Some very fine examples are included here, such as South Hackney County

School, Haggerston Public Baths, Hackney Police Station and Clapton Library. The Edwardian period was also characterised by a boom in entertainment resulting in many cinemas (most of which are now demolished), theatres such as the Hackney Empire, and pubs such as the Adam and Eve in Homerton High Street. During the inter-war period, the main developments included an acceleration in the programme of social housing projects undertaken by the LCC, the boroughs and other philanthropic bodies (e.g. Guinness Trust, Samuel Lewis Trust, etc.) which changed the character of the area greatly. Examples included in this book are the Stamford Hill Estate, Evelyn Court and Lennox House. There were also extensions of 19th century institutions (the German Hospital, the rebuilding of Hackney Town Hall); commercial developments (the Simpson Factory, Bankstock Buildings) and the building of public amenities which helped provide employment in the Depression (the extension of the Piccadilly Line northwards, London Fields Lido).

The postwar dream: scheme for the reconstruction of Shoreditch from the Forshaw-Abercrombie *County of London Plan*, 1943. St. John the Baptist, Hoxton is shown in the centre, and St. Leonard, Shoreditch, bottom right. The main part of this proposal to be executed was the creation of Shoreditch Park on the site of typical 19th century streets.

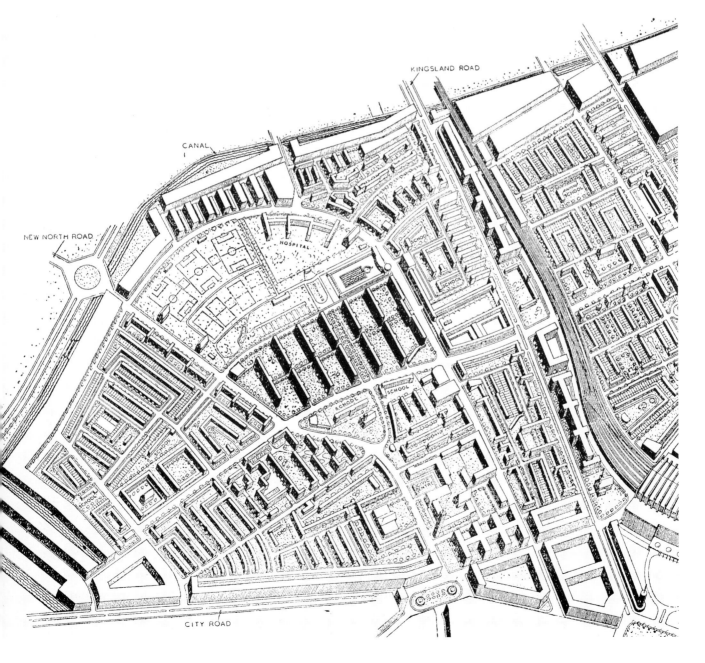

Like all parts of east London, Hackney suffered badly from bombing during the Second World War. Even today, the scars of wartime damage can still be seen. The war provided an opportunity for the implementation of many aspects of the Forshaw-Abercrombie *County of London Plan* of 1941, such as the building of large mixed development estates in response to the acute housing shortage (Woodberry Down, the Somerford Estate). During the postwar period, local authorities had powers of redevelopment which enabled them to build where bombing had taken place, but they could also compulsorily purchase and redevelop whole swathes of terraced housing considered 'unfit for human habitation'. This often led to the destruction of traditional communities, and there are numerous examples where this happened (Hackney Wick with the development of the Trowbridge Estate, Holly Street, Nightingale Estate, the Island, etc.) Hackney contains some of the most experimental, historically significant, and notorious examples of postwar public housing in the country: the full list of every project would be extremely long – only representative examples have been included here such as the pleasantly informal Somerford Estate and the more architecturally domineering Vaine House and Granard House, Gascoyne Estate. Industrial estates were another feature of the 1941 Plan. 'Flatted factories' such as those at Ada Street were built to house small industries, and try to prevent the gradual drift to outer London and resulting loss of employment.

1990s Hackney is both fascinating and confusing. No longer a traditional Labour stronghold, the political situation is far from clear-cut. The borough's proximity to the City of London naturally affects its southernmost parts, in particular Shoreditch and Hoxton. During the 1980s and 90s, Hackney has once more enjoyed a period of popularity with urban professionals, and there have even been some private housing developments such as Sutton Square, marking a return to speculative building not generally seen for a hundred years. In the realm of public housing, right-to-buy legislation has led to a changed picture of ownership. Despite everything, Hackney Council is one of few local authorities building any new council housing in the country, and has initiated some extremely good regeneration projects leading tenants out of a tower block nightmare. Two schemes in particular, Holly Street Estate and Wick Village, have received national acclaim as model projects of their kind, showing how regeneration can produce a fundamental improvement in social and economic conditions.

Alongside the amount of new construction, what has most typified this century has been the growing appreciation of historic architecture. Hackney has seen some of London's most famous conservation battles from the campaign to save the Geffrye Almshouses to more recent cases including the Hackney Empire, Sutton House and the Round Chapel. The number of historic buildings at risk in the borough is still depressingly large compared with other parts of London. But in Hackney as elsewhere there has been a revolution in the appreciation of typical Victorian and Edwardian terraced housing: whole streets and areas, which would have been candidates for redevelopment forty years ago, have been given a new lease of life.

Hackney's 1990s buildings are architecturally very diverse, and some are amongst the most exciting projects in the country. As at the beginning of the century, this diversity reflects a freedom from architectural dogma; in our own time, the loosening of the straitjacket of conventional modernism. The result is that this book starts and ends with particularly interesting projects, and probably no-one would dispute that with recent schemes such as the Geffrye Museum Extension and the new Clissold Sports Centre, Hackney is seeing out the old century on a high architectural note. But, however good the individual buildings, Hackney's abiding problem is the quality of its public realm and its public services. Streets, parks, railway stations, swimming baths, libraries and so on are in a near-disastrous state of repair following years of neglect. Few experiences are as degrading as a ride on the North London Line, or a cycle ride along one of Hackney's numerous pothole-ridden streets. These – as much as its architecture – are the problems which need to be tackled if the urban renaissance that we are promised is to be realised.

Map of Hackney
showing location of buildings discussed

1900-01
1 Hackney Empire Theatre,
291 Mare Street, E8
Frank Matcham

1902
2 South Hackney County
School,
Cassland Road, E9
T J Bailey

1902
3 The Shannon Factory,
Tyssen Street, Dalston, E8
Edwin Sachs

1904
4 Haggerston Public Baths,
Whiston Road, E2
Alfred W S Cross

1904
5 Police Station,
2-4 Lower Clapton Road, E5
John Dixon Butler

1905-07
6 London County Council
Electricity Substation,
6-8 Garden Walk,
Shoreditch, EC2
E Vincent Harris

1909-11
7 St. Barnabas Church,
Shacklewell Row, E8
Charles Reilly

1912
8 Canal Bridge,
New North Road/Regent's
Canal, Hoxton, N1
engineer: T L Hustler

1913-14
9 Clapton Library,
Northwold Road, E5
Edwin Cooper

1914-15
10 The New Synagogue,
Egerton Road,
Stamford Hill, N16
Ernest M Joseph

1929/1933-34
11 The Simpson Factory,
92-100 Stoke Newington
Road, Shacklewell, N16
*Hobden & Porri/Burnett
& Eprile*

1931-39
12 Stamford Hill Estate,
Stamford Hill, N16
*London County Council
Architect's Dept*

1932
13 London Fields Lido,
London Fields, E8
*possibly H A Rowbotham
& T L Smithson*

1932
14 Manor House
Underground Station,
Green Lanes/Seven Sisters
Road, N4
Charles Holden

1933-34
15 Evelyn Court,
Amhurst Road, E8
Burnet, Tait & Lorne

1935-36
16 The German Hospital,
East Wing, Fassett Square, E8
Burnet, Tait & Lorne

1934-37
17 Hackney Town Hall and
Municipal Offices,
Mare Street, E8
Lanchester & Lodge

1937
18 Lennox House,
Cresset Road, E9
J E M MacGregor

1937
19 The Rio Cinema,
107 Kingsland High Street,
Dalston, E8
Frederick E Bromige

1935-37
20 Stoke Newington Civic
Centre,
Stoke Newington Church
Street, N16
J Reginald Truelove

1938-39
21 Bankstock Buildings,
42-44 De Beauvoir Crescent,
N1
Robert Sharp

1947-48
22 Brett Manor,
Brett Road, E8
Edward Mills

1946-49
23 Somerford Estate,
Shacklewell Road, N16
*Frederick Gibberd with
G L Downing*

1946-52
24 Woodberry Down Estate,
Manor House, N4
London County Council

1947-49/1966-67
25 Benthal Schools,
Benthal Road, Stoke
Newington, N16
*London County Council
Architect's Dept/Greater
London Council Architect's
Dept (Paul Maas)*

1950
26 Wilton Estate,
Lansdowne Drive, E8
Norman & Dawbarn

1949-52
27 John Scott Health Centre
and Nursery School,
Green Lanes, N4
*London County Council
Architect's Dept*

1955
28 Vaine House & Granard
House, Gascoyne Estate,
Hartlake Road, E9
*London County Council
Architect's Dept*

1958
29 The Beckers,
Rectory Road, N16
*Frederick Gibberd with
G L Downing*

1959-60
30 St. Michael & All Angels
Church,
Lansdowne Drive, London
Fields, E8
N F Cachemaille-Day

1958-61
31 Kingsgate Estate,
Tottenham Road,
De Beauvoir, N1
*Frederick Gibberd with G L
Downing*

1961-62
32 Lion Boys' Club,
148-152 Pitfield Street,
Hoxton, N1
Francis Pollen

1963-65
33 Haggerston Girls' School,
Weymouth Terrace, E2
*Ernö Goldfinger and Hubert
Bennett*

1965-66
34 Ada Street Workshops,
Ada Street, E8
*Yorke, Rosenberg & Mardall
with Hubert Bennett*

1969-77
35 Christchurch Estate,
Victoria Park Road, E9
John Spence & Partners

1972
36 Ickburgh School,
Ickburgh Road, Clapton, E5
Foster Associates

1981-84
37 Social housing,
Church Crescent, E9
Colquhoun & Miller

1984
38 Social housing,
Shrubland Road, Albion
Drive and Brownlow Road, E8
Colquhoun & Miller

1983-84
39 Sutton Square,
Urswick Road, E9
CZWG

1980-87
40 Homerton Hospital and
Education Centre,
Homerton Grove, E9
YRM Architects & Planners

1991-94
41 Schonfeld Square,
Lordship Road, Stoke
Newington, N16
Hunt Thompson Associates

1995
42 Garden gazebo,
Albion Square, E8
David French

1993-95
43 Wick Village,
Hackney Wick, E9
Levitt Bernstein Associates

1995-96
44 Rushton Street Surgeries,
Hoxton, N1
Penoyre & Prasad

1992-97/1998-99
45 Hackney Community
College, Shoreditch Campus,
Falkirk Street, Hoxton, N1
*Hampshire County Architects
& Perkins Ogden Architects*

1997
46 Lux Building,
Hoxton Square, N1
Macreanor Lavington

1996-98
47 The Geffrye Museum
Extension,
Kingsland Road, E2
*Branson Coates (with
Sheppard Robson)*

1988-98
48 Private housing,
1 Truman's Road,
Shacklewell, N16
Cullinan & Harbour

1998-99
49 Social housing,
Murray Grove, Hoxton, N1
Cartwright Pickard

1998-
50 Clissold Sports Centre,
Clissold Road, Stoke
Newington, N16
Hodder Associates

I Hackney Empire Theatre

291 Mare Street, E8

DATE   1900–01
ARCHITECT   Frank Matcham
CLIENT   Moss Empires Ltd

bingo session in full swing, 1965

Opposite Hackney
Empire Theatre in 1901

Hackney Empire: the statue of
Euterpe, goddess of lyric music,
awaits erection on top of the rebuilt
pediment. This replacement statue,
based on the original of 1901, was
made by Shaws of Darwen,
Lancashire. August 1988

The Hackney Empire was built in the midst of the Edwardian boom in theatre building. It was a response to demand from those who did not want, or could not afford to travel into central London for entertainment.

The theatrical entrepreneur Oswald Stoll formed a partnership with Edward Moss in 1895. Stoll strove to provide high-class entertainment in establishments built to the highest architectural standards. His collaboration with the architect Frank Matcham (1854-1920) began in the mid-1890s. Matcham's output consisted almost entirely of theatres – about 150 new or substantially remodelled buildings, including the London Coliseum, Buxton Opera House, Grand Theatre Blackpool and the Belfast Opera House. The hallmarks of his style are eye-catching exteriors, good acoustics, clear sight-lines, safe circulation spaces and exits, and a generous stage; above all, a sense of intimacy between performer and audience, and of theatrical enchantment, which fulfilment of the basic requirements could never alone have achieved. The Hackney Empire exemplifies all these stylistic traits in grand style, and on a grand scale, with a seating capacity of 2,500. A 1998 survey by the Theatres Trust placed it in the top 45 UK theatres outside the West End 'of the highest theatrical quality'.

Despite the huge success of his theatres, Matcham's work did not meet with professional approval during his lifetime. Authorities such as Edwin Sachs (see p. 20) cited the grand Neoclassical opera houses and theatres of central Europe in preference to the commercial flamboyance of Matcham and his contemporaries. It is only in the last 10 years that Matcham's work has really come to be appreciated.

The Hackney Empire Palace Ltd was floated in December 1900 with a share capital of £50,000 and debenture stock of £26,000. The theatre opened a year later. Coming to the footlights at the end of the show, Stoll confided to his audience that people had told the directors that the hall was too good for Hackney, but it was his opinion that 'nothing was too good for Hackney'. The Empire proved to be a successful business enterprise, remaining so until after the Second World War. It was converted in 1956 for studio productions by ATV Ltd, and was acquired by Mecca Ltd in 1961 for use as a bingo hall. During the bingo era, a number of degrading alterations were made, including painting over the original decorative scheme. Now that the Empire is successfully back in use as a variety theatre, its original character is gradually being restored, and plans are being drawn up (architect, Tim Ronalds) to make major improvements to the theatre's back-of-stage area and other facilities by integrating the theatre with two adjacent sites.

The exterior is in ornate Baroque style, of red brick and buff terracotta, with a three-bay façade. The elaborate twin terracotta domes and pediment were removed in 1979, but replaced in 1988 following a public inquiry which required their reinstatement in the original material. The auditorium is large, with opulent plasterwork and painted decoration throughout. There are three tiers, of which the lower two stretch round to embrace the side boxes. The balconies are supported on steel cantilevers, permitting the clear sight-lines for which Matcham was famous. The auditorium roof was designed to open, but it is a long time since that mechanism has been put to use.

South Hackney County School

Cassland Road, E9

DATE	1902
ARCHITECT	T J Bailey
CLIENT	London School Board

This school was designed as a girls' school by T J Bailey and opened on 25 August 1902. It has remained in educational use for almost a century, most recently as part of Hackney Sixth Form Centre.

The 1870 Education Act provided the impetus for London to lead the way in school building, and as a result the London School Board was formed in 1871 to build schools for public education. The Board functioned until 1904, when the London County Council took over this responsibility. Over 550 schools were designed in the period from 1871 to 1910. South Hackney County School is therefore part of the remarkable architectural phenomenon of Board Schools built in London. Soon after its formation the Board appointed an architect; the position was first held by E R Robson, who was assisted by Bailey as chief draughtsman from 1873. In 1884 Bailey succeeded Robson as architect, working there until well into the LCC era in 1910. This continuity resulted in buildings which are recognisably in 'Board School Style', an institutional variant of the Queen Anne style, using tall white sash windows within gabled brick façades.

T J Bailey (1843-1910) and his team were therefore responsible for designing enormous numbers of schools. South Hackney County School is one of the grander designs from the last decade of his career, specially designed because it was one of the first examples of an exclusively secondary school. It is an impressive building, a virtuoso essay in Edwardian opulence, combining power and grandeur with beautiful detailing. The school is two storeys high, of red brick with terracotta decoration. In the bold front elevation each part of the plan is expressed as a separate architectural unit in the symmetrical rhythm A B C D C B A. This pattern is reminiscent of Baroque layouts and was often used by Bailey. Here the focal point of the layout is the centrally-placed hall of four bays with pitched roof. The terracotta is very fine, including window architraves and rounded window surrounds with swirling ornamentation, deep cornice, pilasters and urns with swags of fruit.

The School Board published a *Final Report* in 1904 summarising its ideals: 'The policy of the School Board has almost always been to give these buildings, as public buildings, some dignity of appearance, and make them ornaments rather than disfigurements to the neighbourhoods in which they are erected ... It was found that the difference of cost between bare utilitarianism and buildings designed in some sort of style and with regard for materials and colour, was rather less than 5%. At the same time, this ornamental appearance may be secured either by richness of detail, or by a dignified grouping of masses; it is the policy of

South Hackney County School

the Board, while studying, in the first instance, suitable arrangements for teaching, not to set aside the dignity and attractiveness of buildings which the Board have always felt should be a contrast to their poor surroundings.'

South Hackney County School makes a distinguished contribution to the streetscape, but is being converted into loft appartments following its recent sale for redevelopment. Further education in the borough has been rationalised since the opening of Hackney Community College in 1997, resulting in several redundant buildings.

The Shannon Factory

(now Springfield House)
Tyssen Street, Dalston, E8

DATE	1902
ARCHITECT	Edwin Sachs
CLIENT	The Shannon Company Ltd

The Shannon Factory: an engraving published in *The Building News*, 26 September 1902

This large building, tucked away off Dalston Lane, is well worth exploration. It was designed for the Shannon Company, cabinet makers for offices and banks, by Edwin Sachs. Even by today's standards, the building is impressively large, with three linked blocks in the form of a U ranged around a cobbled courtyard. It is 77 ft. high with five storeys. It is easily the most important 20th century industrial building in Hackney.

Edwin Sachs (1870-1919) was something of a polymath and a man of considerable energies. Born in London of German parents, he studied architecture in Berlin, specialising in the study of government buildings. Early on he became fascinated by the relationship between architecture, fire prevention and building legislation, working with the Berlin Fire Brigade in order to gain a better understanding of the causes of fire. He returned to London and set up in practice in Waterloo Place. At the age of just 26 he wrote *Modern Opera Houses and Theatres* (1896-98), a magnificent work

describing theatres all over the world, and in particular their structure and stage machinery. His architectural output was small and almost exclusively in the realm of theatre: stages for two existing theatres, the Drury Lane Theatre (1898) and the Royal Opera House, Covent Garden (1899-1901), an unexecuted commission to remodel the opera house in Cairo and design work on the Grand Theatre, Llandudno. The Shannon Factory is his only surviving complete building. In 1897 he founded the British Fire Prevention Committee which began to analyse the relationship between fire and construction techniques. At the Committee's Testing Station, he carried out experiments on building materials of every kind. He realised the importance to fire prevention of construction in reinforced concrete, a material which was taken up considerably later in Britain than on the continent. To help promote the use of concrete, he founded the periodical *Concrete and Constructional Engineering* in 1906 and remained its editor until his death.

The Shannon Company were cabinet makers specialising in furnishings for offices and banks, manufactured under licence from their American parent company. The site they chose for their new factory was alongside part of the North London Railway at Dalston, and had previously been occupied by terraced housing for the poor, according to Booth's Map of 1889. The brief was drawn up by Mr Schaefer, the Managing Director, and it seems obvious that he went to Sachs as his architect because of his expertise in fire prevention and the building regulations. However, this was more than just a utilitarian project: Sachs was pleased to exhibit two of his designs for the

The Shannon Factory: ground plan, drawn December 1901

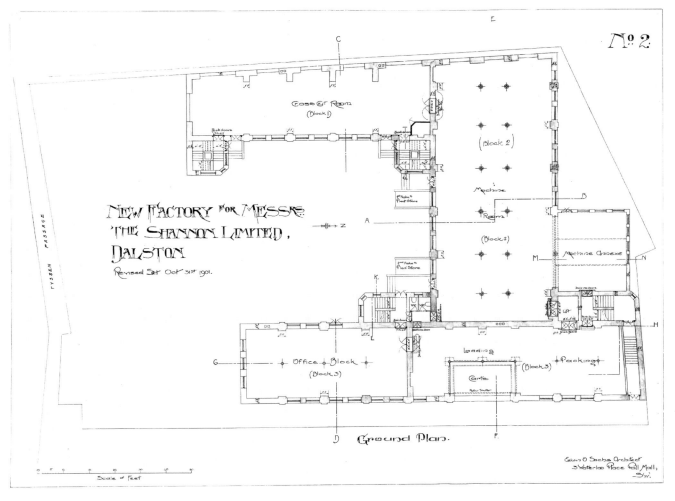

factory at the Royal Academy in 1902-3 (the second submitted in the names of both Sachs and G S Hoffman, his partner) and to have it illustrated in *The Building News*, 26 September 1902. Under the London Building Act of 1894, the London County Council could refuse planning permission for any space exceeding 250,000 cubic ft. if the manufacturing process involved the use of inflammable materials. Schaefer wanted to base the layout of the factory on the latest American models. He asked for a large, undivided space of over 400,000 cubic ft. in Block 2, the central block of the factory, in order to introduce semi-automated methods of manufacture using lengths of wood up to 18 ft. placed on end. Because of this it was essential to have room heights of over 20 ft. The company also wished to have the polishing room, using inflammable materials, in the same block. It was these points which took Sachs, the LCC Architect and the Metropolitan Fire Brigade over a year to resolve. Sachs made five applications for planning permission. By the time this was granted in January 1902, a whole range of additional fire prevention measures had been incorporated into the design. The polishing room had been moved to one of the side blocks; the central block was built using the latest fire protection techniques; electric lighting was used instead of gas; central heating was introduced instead of open fires; a full sprinkler system was installed and a direct telephone link to the Fire Station was included. With each revised application Sachs submitted a complete set of drawings, which demonstrate his detailed involvement with every stage of the project.

The building that was eventually built following these negotiations had essentially two different forms of construction. The side wings had floors consisting of steel beams and timber joists with pugging between the joists. At the wider spans, the floors were supported by cast iron columns. By

The Shannon Factory: various elevations to the courtyard, drawn December 1901

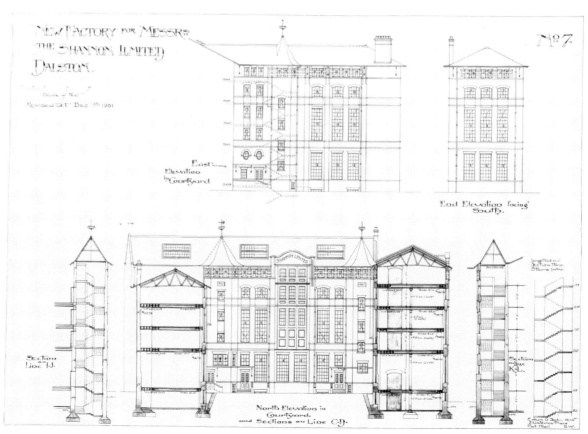

contrast, the central machine room block had steel columns and beams supporting Columbian fire-proof floors. This proprietary system, which was tested by the British Fire Prevention Committee, consisted of steel-ribbed bars embedded in concrete. For double protection the underside of the floors was protected with Uralite slabs. The builders were Howard & Co of Covent Garden. Fire-resistant doors and iron casement windows were made by Crittall. Externally, simple materials such as stock brick and plain red facings were used effectively, giving the building a continental feel. The three main stone staircases are marked with distinctive turrets (only one turret survives intact), adding a certain panache to the overall effect. Two of these incorporate terracotta panels bearing the text AD 1902. A separate building at the entrance to the courtyard contained the boiler and engine houses. The courtyard retains its original cobble stones. The centre block was for cabinet-making, with the ground floor used for machinery and the large room on the first floor for joining up large sections of cabinet work. The west block contained sawing machinery, and the east block offices and the polishing shop. The fact that the building was designed from the inside out results in its unusually interesting appearance.

Despite the efforts put into designing the building, the Shannon Company only occupied the whole building for a short time. There may have been a slump in demand for furniture, for by 1906 the freehold of the buildings had been acquired by Marconi's Wireless & Telegraph Company, and The Shannon retreated to Block 1 and the second floors of Blocks 2 and 3. Siemens also used the building from 1908 to 1963, and from 1965 to 1972 it was used by AEI as stores. (Both the names Siemens and AEI can be seen on the water tower above the building.) From 1979 it has been called Springfield House, and has been used by a number of small businesses and organisations since then. Its robustness has ensured that it has survived for almost a century, and it has adapted to divided use.

lan of the west elevation to the ourtyard, drawn December 1901

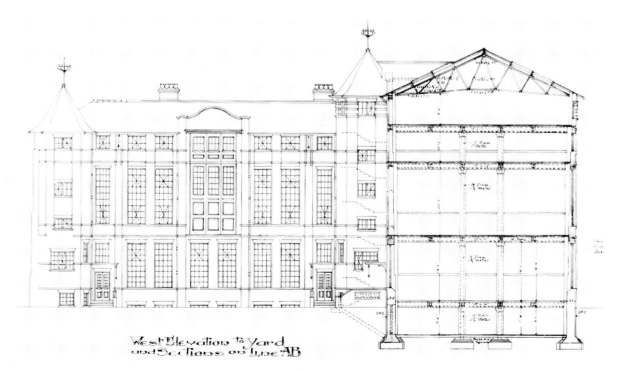

West Elevation to Yard
and Sections on line AB

4 Haggerston Public Baths

Whiston Road, E2

DATE	1904
ARCHITECT	Alfred W S Cross
CLIENT	Shoreditch Borough Council

Haggerston Baths is a splendid example of Edwardian municipal enterprise at its best. The provision of public baths and wash-houses started in the 1840s at the height of the Victorian anxiety about public health and sanitation. In London the first baths were built by charities established for the purpose, but soon an Act of Parliament was passed allowing local authorities to build baths and wash-houses on the rates. By the end of the century there was a broad consensus about the provision and arrangement of public baths, and architects such as Alfred Cross developed a special expertise in producing suitable designs. He was sufficiently proud of Haggerston Baths to illustrate it as an exemplary project in his book *Public Baths and Wash Houses* (1906).

Haggerston Public Baths:
the men's and women's entrances
in Whiston Road, c1910

Haggerston Public Baths: the opening ceremony on 25 June 1904

Even those who have never used the baths will know the building for its fine façade, topped by a cupola surmounted by a gilded ship which can be seen from many surrounding streets. The building is two storeys with cellars and attics, built of red brick and Portland stone. Below the pedimented main elevation are the men's and women's entrances with elaborately carved stone doorways incorporating lions rampant – the Shoreditch Borough coat-of-arms. The rear elevation towards the canal is equally impressive.

Cross took great care over the layout of the building. At the time, swimming baths usually included slipper (or warm) baths since many households had no bath – councils were keen to provide opportunities for cleanliness as well as exercise. The grand main entrances led to a ticket office. To the left were the men's slipper baths, straight ahead the swimming pool, and to the right the women's slipper baths. The splendid entrances are no longer in use, which gives the building a derelict feel. The present utilitarian entrance is tucked away on the west side of the building, and the original ticket hall is just an empty space. The ground floor also contained a public laundry and club room. The basement contained the boiler house, coal store, engineer's workshop and many other functions.

There is a single 100 ft. swimming pool, which has unfortunately been divided to provide a learning pool, thus reducing the overall length for serious swimming. The pool is top lit, with an attractive curved steel-framed roof. Half the slipper (or warm) baths remain and there has been some internal re-arrangement to provide gym facilities.

The baths were opened with due pomp by the Mayor of Shoreditch on 25 June 1904, when the Vice Chairman of the Baths Committee, Alderman E J Wakeling swam the length of the bath under water. Today the building survives as an immensely useful facility, still fulfilling most of Alfred Cross's original intentions. However, it is in dire need of sympathetic refurbishment. It is one of few swimming baths in the borough (the others are at King's Hall and Britannia Leisure Centres; another is under construction at Clissold Road.)

⑤ Police Station

2-4 Lower Clapton Road, E5

DATE	1904
ARCHITECT	John Dixon Butler
CLIENT	Metropolitan Police

This building is typical of early 20th century London police stations, which were all designed by John Dixon Butler, the Metropolitan Police architect. At the turn of the century, three types of public building were being produced to a standardised type of design; schools, police stations and underground stations. Our ideas of what a typical police station looks like date from this period, and the one in Lower Clapton Road is a very good example of its kind. Also in Hackney, Butler designed the station in Dalston Lane (now converted into Cape House Hostel).

John Dixon Butler (1861-1920) was Architect and Surveyor to the Metropolitan Police from 1895 until his death, and designed over 200 police stations and magistrates' courts. These include many well-known London police stations ranging from small suburban stations to larger, more flamboyant ensembles such as Shoreditch at Old Street, Harrow and Tower Bridge. He was adept at planning the internal layout of police stations and went on to assist Richard Norman Shaw in designing New Scotland Yard in 1904.

The Lower Clapton Road Police Station, a familiar part of the central Hackney streetscape, was built in 1904 on the site of a pair of semi-detached late Georgian villas. Similar villas remain to the east. The station is on the corner of Lower Clapton Road and St. John-at-Hackney Churchyard. Prior to this, the Police Station was across the churchyard in the end terraced house which is now 422 Mare Street.

The building contains cells, offices and a section house. It has three storeys, plus an attic storey in the mansard roof and a semi-basement. It is built of red brick with stone dressings. The main façade has five bays, with a central doorcase of stone. The side wall gables contain very tall chimneys, a device frequently used by Butler. At the front, there are cast iron railings to areas and a Windsor blue glass lantern marked 'Police'. The distinctive central stone doorcase with its hood is one of the hallmarks of the architect's style, which was strongly influenced by the Arts and Crafts movement. A plaque in the east wall bears the inscription 'Property of the Receiver for Metropolitan Police. 1904'.

Hackney Police Station, 1906

6 London County Council Electricity Substation

(now The Tramshed)
6-8 Garden Walk, Shoreditch, EC2

DATE 1905-07
ARCHITECT E Vincent Harris
CLIENT London County Council

This handsome building at the corner of Garden Walk and Rivington Street, built as a substation to serve the London County Council tramway system, is a gem of municipal architecture. It was designed in 1905 by E Vincent Harris, and is one of only three substations of its type remaining in London. It is a strong, vigorous building in a muscular Edwardian Baroque style.

The terms on which tramways had been built in London allowed for their purchase by the local authority after a fixed term, and once the LCC had been

London County Council
Electricity Substation, 1998

established in 1889 it began to show an interest in exercising its power to take them over. Most of the tramways south of the river were transferred to the LCC in 1899; those north of the river were taken over seven years later.

As it acquired the tramways, the LCC set in action a programme for their electrification including the building of Greenwich generating station, the first part of which was completed in 1906. North of the river, the routes along Old Street and Bethnal Green Road and up Kingsland Road to Stoke Newington were electrified early in 1907. It was to serve these and other routes beyond the City that the Shoreditch substation was built. Through it the 6,600 volts AC transmitted from the generating station was reduced to 550 volts DC for operating the trams. The transformers were on the main floor and the switchgear in the basement.

The design and construction of the substation were treated as 'in-house' projects by the LCC; the architect was E Vincent Harris, and construction was carried out by the LCC Works Department. Harris (1879-1971) started his career as an LCC architect working on several electricity generating stations before setting up in private practice. His other surviving London substations are in Upper Street, Islington (now transformed into the famous Mall Antiques Arcade) and in Arlington Road, Camden. He subsequently achieved fame as one of the most dedicated exponents of the Classical Revival, and designed some notable public buildings including Sheffield City Hall (1932) and the Civic Hall, Leeds (1933).

The building is constructed of brick, using rustication to replicate the Baroque style. This gives both refinement and solidity which have won the building many admirers. The giant rusticated pilasters which flank the Rivington Street doorway are particularly striking. Portland stone copings are used round doorways, window cills and at parapet level. The sheer quality of design illustrates the LCC's pride in its public buildings. The building is now known as The Tramshed, and is used as a furniture warehouse.

7 St. Barnabas Church

Shacklewell Row, E8

DATE	1909-11
ARCHITECT	Charles Reilly
CLIENT	Merchant Taylors' School Mission

This quietly impressive church is tucked away inside a triangle of housing formed by Shacklewell Row, Shacklewell Lane and Seal Street, and can only be approached by a passage at the side of the church hall. The exceedingly built-up location means that the church is hidden by high buildings and can barely be seen from any of the surrounding streets. However, it is one of the hidden gems of Hackney, and one of the best churches of its date in London.

Charles Reilly (1874-1948) combined architectural practice with academic teaching as head of the Liverpool School of Architecture. His architectural output was small. His most significant buildings include the Students' Union at Liverpool University, Liverpool Playhouse and the church of St. Barnabas in Shacklewell, an early work.

The church was built to serve the Merchant Taylors' School missionary work in north-east London. Reilly grew up in Stoke Newington and attended

St. Barnabas Church, 1993

the school (then in the city) and the mission church. This is doubtless how he came to be appointed to design the new building. The foundation stone was laid on 3 July 1909, and the building opened the following year. It seats 400. The church hall, which was originally the school mission, dates from *c*1889, well before there was a church on the site. St. Barnabas is the daughter church of West Hackney church (St. Paul's) on Stoke Newington Road (bombed in the Second World War and rebuilt). It was not consecrated as the parish church of Shacklewell until 1929.

The church is in an unusual round arched, basilica style. It is built in an interesting combination of stock brick and reinforced concrete. In particular, the barrel vaulted nave and the crossing dome are of concrete with the ribs faced in brick. At this time reinforced concrete was still used almost exclusively for industrial buildings, so St. Barnabas is an unusually early use in an ecclesiastical context. The construction was felt to be sufficiently interesting for it to be featured in the technical journal, *Concrete*, as the building work progressed. Originally, the choir screen of four Roman doric columns supported a simple wooden cross. However Reilly's involvement with the building continued and in 1936 the screen was completed with the addition of a rood, made by the Liverpool sculptor Herbert Tyson Smith and gilded and painted at Reilly's own expense. The interior is restrained and impressive, a good example of a building in a single style. Reilly wrote in 1938 that he wished to be remembered by this building.

Photograph showing the nave roof and dome nearing completion. From the periodical *Concrete*, 1911

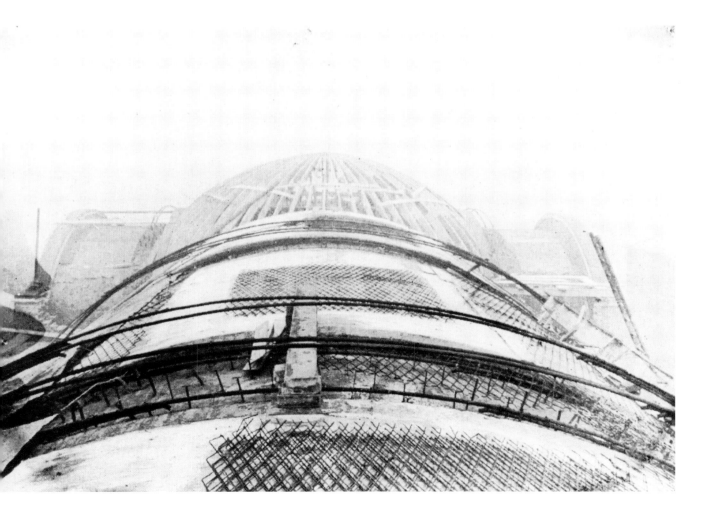

⑧ Canal Bridge

New North Road/Regent's Canal, Hoxton, N1

DATE   1912
ENGINEER   T L Hustler
CLIENT   Shoreditch Borough Council

The technique of reinforced concrete construction was known about in Britain in the mid-1850s, but was not widely used until the 1890s. The main reason for its eventual adoption was the successful promotion of the technique by the Frenchman François Hennebique. He devised a particular system of reinforcement, which was allowed to be used only by contractors operating under licence. A fellow French engineer, L G Mouchel, became his British agent in 1897 and was largely responsible for the fact that about two-thirds of early reinforced concrete structures in the UK were on the Hennebique system.

Where Hackney is concerned, the most important Hennebique monument is this bridge on the New North Road crossing the Regent's Canal, which survives as testimony to the durability of his system. Its overall design was by the Borough Engineer for Shoreditch, and it was built by Higgs & Hill Ltd (presumably one of the contractors that Hennebique had licensed). The introduction of trams on the New North Road seems to have been the reason for rebuilding the bridge over the canal and the weight of the trams demanded a particularly robust design. This was achieved by using the tall parapets of the bridge as part of the longitudinal strengthening.

A similar bridge had been built over the Haggerston Basin off Whiston Road in 1911, also a Shoreditch Borough project. That bridge has now been demolished so the New North Road bridge can claim to be the earliest of its kind in the Borough, if not in London as a whole. It may not be an object of great beauty, but technically it is a remarkable survival.

Canal bridge at New North Road crossing the Regent's Canal, 1998

⑨ Clapton Library

Northwold Road, E5

DATE   1913–14
ARCHITECT   Edwin Cooper
CLIENT   Hackney Borough Council

The distinguished Edwardian architect Edwin Cooper designed three libraries in Hackney: Dalston (1913, destroyed 1945), Homerton (1912–13, now Chats Palace Arts Centre) and the Clapton Library. This period was an active one for building libraries throughout London and further afield, for several reasons. From the mid-19th century legislation enabled public libraries to be built, but it was not until two private benefactors, John Passmore Edwards and Andrew Carnegie, provided funds for building libraries that the legislation was really put to work. The council adopted the Public Libraries Act in 1903, first acquiring land in Mare Street where the

Clapton Library:
the opening ceremony
on Saturday 17 January 1914

Central Library, built with funds from Carnegie, was opened in 1908. Branch libraries in Dalston, Homerton and Clapton followed. Carnegie (1835-1919) was born in Scotland, but emigrated and made his fortune in heavy industry in the United States. By 1919, 2,800 libraries worldwide had been established through his generosity, including Clapton Library. Over half the libraries in Britain received some funds from Carnegie. The period from 1885 to 1914 was therefore a boom time for library building, and many of the designs were of very high architectural quality, both to inspire the readers and to bring a measure of dignity to poorer areas.

Land in Northwold Road was purchased at a cost of £750 in May 1912, and plans were adopted in July that year and forwarded to Carnegie for his approval. The estimated cost was £5,280.

A typical library of this period had open access shelves, a lending department, newspaper room, magazine room and reference department. The newspaper and magazine rooms provided a chance for people to keep abreast of contemporary events at a time when newspapers were still relatively expensive. Originally at Clapton Library the ground floor contained the juveniles' reading room and a combined news, magazine and reading room, together with vestibule, entrance hall and staff rooms; the first floor housed the lending library in a galleried room above the main reading room. This design also enabled the library to be staffed by just two librarians.

Clapton Library is two storeys high, built of red brickwork with tiles. The front elevation is extremely wide, with a large arch made from tiles placed on end interspersed with brick at each end. The window surrounds are of rubbed brickwork demonstrating the excellent quality of bricklaying. There is a handsome cornice and hipped roof tiled with slate. The style is English Renaissance, the style and type of brickwork echoing that found in the work of Wren and his contemporaries. There are stone panels above each arch, complementing the brickwork, and incorporating the name of the building and an owl (indicating learning and wisdom). The design of the building allowed for as much natural light inside as possible. The open gallery above the main reading room was infilled in the early 1970s to create a complete first floor, which is now a children's library. The false ceiling has both lowered the height of the ground floor room and ruined its proportions. The single storey back room was originally top lit, with a ceiling incorporating an elegant combination of leaded lights and leaf mouldings. This too has been obscured by a false ceiling.

The library was refurbished externally in 1998. Throughout the borough, libraries have suffered from lack of funding, and also from a feeling that older library buildings are unsuitable for modern use. But buildings of this quality are worthy of conservation, not least because the role they were designed to play is still vitally important.

⑩ The New Synagogue

Egerton Road, Stamford Hill, N16

DATE   1914–15
ARCHITECT Ernest M Joseph
CLIENT   Trustees of the United Synagogue

This building is closely related to an earlier building, the New Synagogue of 1837–38 which stood in Great St. Helen's, Bishopsgate. That synagogue had originated as one of three 18th century Ashkenazi synagogues in the City of London. By the end of the 19th century many members of its congregation had moved to new homes north-east of the City. In response to that change, in 1912 the United Synagogue Council decided to build a new synagogue in Egerton Road, Stamford Hill, at the heart of the Jewish community which had settled there. The sale of the old Bishopsgate site easily provided enough funding for the new building.

The Egerton Road synagogue and neighbouring school were designed in 1913 by Ernest M Joseph of Joseph & Smithem. His design is close to that of the original St. Helen's building, so much so that it has been described by some as a 're-erection'. However, its main elevation is a characteristically Edwardian Baroque composition, with its Doric portico and two domed

The New Synagogue, 1989

The magnificent interior of the
New Synagogue, 1989

towers flanking the central pediment. The interior also has an Edwardian
opulence, but is closer in spirit to the 1830s building on which it was
modelled. The galleried space, with barrel-vaulted ceiling, leads towards the
apse which is marked by paired Corinthian columns. Lunettes within the
ceiling help create a light, airy space. Many of the fittings including the
pulpit, central bimah, candelabra, silverware, the Ark and stained glass were
brought from the old building.

The New Synagogue was opened on 21 March 1915. Situated in the
flourishing middle-class Jewish area of Stamford Hill, it was well-attended
and prosperous for several decades until the Second World War. It was one
of the focal points of Jewish religious and communal life in north London.
Ashkenazi Jews supported the synagogue until the mid-1970s, by which time
the middle-class Jewish population had moved further out, and a growing
minority of Chasidic Jews had settled in the area. They traditionally favour
schtieblach (small synagogues often found in private houses), rather than
synagogues which are large and cathedral-like. Despite this, the United
Synagogue sold the New Synagogue, its oldest establishment, to a Chasidic
group, the Bobov Community, in 1987.

The Simpson Factory

(now Halkevi Community Centre and Hays Information Management)
92-100 Stoke Newington Road, Shacklewell, N16

DATE 1929 (Somerford Grove extension 1933-34)
ARCHITECTS Hobden & Porri (1929 building)
Burnett & Eprile (1933 Somerford Grove extension)
CLIENT S Simpson Ltd

This large building in Stoke Newington Road tantalisingly retains lettering which reads 'Established 1894. Built 1929. The House of — '. The missing word is Simpson, the famous clothing manufacturer and retailer. Simeon Simpson (1878-1932) began tailoring in the late 1890s in Houndsditch in the City. By the 1920s his company had several workshops including ones at Middlesex Street, off Aldgate, the City Road and other locations on the fringes of the City. It was felt that consolidation in a single, large manufacturing premises was desirable and the company embarked on this major building project in Hackney. As well as running one of the most successful British clothing companies, Simpson made time for a considerable amount of voluntary work in the area, and was a Councillor for the Clapton

The Simpson Factory. The front elevation on Stoke Newington Road, facing west, 1935

38

Park Ward of Hackney from 1926 to 1928. During the 1920s he lived at 124 Bethune Road, Stoke Newington.

Simeon Simpson acquired several houses at 92-100 Stoke Newington Road in 1925, and the architects Hobden & Porri were engaged to design a new factory there. They were a practice specialising in industrial, commercial and public buildings including the handsome Egyptian-influenced Britannia House at 231-233 Shaftesbury Avenue (1929). More locally, in Stoke Newington, they designed the War Memorial entrance to the Library in Stoke Newington Church Street (1923) and the Clissold Road swimming baths (1930, demolished 1997). Porri was particularly interested in achieving as much light as possible in industrial and commercial premises, which often led to conflict with the planning authorities. Their buildings can be described as industrial Art Deco in style.

The 1929 building is three storeys with a steel frame and reinforced concrete floors. The west elevation facing Stoke Newington Road and a short return on Somerford Grove are of artificial stone. Square-cut columns in the stonework extend from ground to second floor giving the building a feeling of solidity, and emphasising its scale. On the main façade the windows are double height extending from the ground floor to the first. The remainder of the Somerford Grove elevation is of buff stock brick with white cement-rendered piers, artifical stone mullions, with the wall at ground floor level of brown salt-glazed bricks. On the ground floor, the front section of the building was used for offices, storage, packing and despatch and the rear section for pressers and inspectors. Here, large windows extended to sill level on the first floor. The first floor was used for trouser and vest making, and the second floor as a cutting room.

The Simpson Factory. Somerford Grove extension looking towards Stoke Newington Road after bombing in September 1940. The houses on the right were demolished to make way for Gibberd's Somerford Estate, built 1946-49

By 1930, business was clearly booming, as Simpson wanted to extend the factory to the south, adding a storey to the Somerford Grove side. Ancient lights agreements were negotiated with the Metropolitan Police, who owned the neighbouring property in Stoke Newington Road, and the owners of properties at 1 to 7 Somerford Grove. However, these minor extensions proved insufficient to meet the demand for more space. By 1933 Simpson had acquired numbers 2-16 on the south side of Somerford Grove, and engaged another firm of architects, Burnett & Eprile, to design a sizeable extension. It was said that the new wing would provide employment for 1,000 people. The extension was even higher than the original building, with four storeys and a basement.

Burnett and Eprile were partners from 1923 until 1939. Burnett's particular speciality was advising on the legalities surrounding ancient lights, and he may have been engaged for his expertise on this subject given the considerable size of the Somerford Grove extension. There were objections from neighbouring Shacklewell School, which were eventually resolved. Opposite the factory extension, the semi-detached villas remained until after the Second World War. Because of war damage, they were demolished, making way for Gibberd's post-war Somerford Estate of 1946-49 (see p. 67).

The façade of the extension is of quite different materials – red stock brick, with bands of faience between each floor. A faience panel on the 1934 extension wall lists Burnett & Eprile as architects, Higgs & Hill as contractors and Shaws as the faience manufacturers. As with the main building, the extension has a steel frame and concrete floors. Two very grand entrances have attractive teak doors recessed in faience doorways, perhaps more suited to a Thirties cinema than a factory. Each floor was planned as completely undivided space. There was deal flooring throughout.

The extended factory covered almost 200,000 square ft., and employed over 3,000 people. At the height of production, 11,000 garments were made per day. The building was described as a model factory, highly regarded throughout the clothing industry as the most advanced of its kind. Both Simeon Simpson and his son Alexander travelled widely, and the design of the factory was undoubtedly influenced by American and continental examples. In 1935, the DAKS brand was developed at the Stoke Newington factory – a revolutionary new style of casual trousers, in different weights of cloth and colours, with a new cut of waist band which did not require belt or braces! The slogan was 'comfort in action'. These were an instant success, partly because of the clever use of aspirational and educational marketing, and also because customers had increased leisure time when more casual clothing could be worn. The success of this brand enabled the company to finance the building of its flagship shop at Piccadilly, which opened in 1936.

The Simpson company vacated the building in 1981. The front building is now used by the Turkish community as the Halkevi Community Centre, and the side extension for document storage. The scale of the building is testimony to a period of economic vitality which can scarcely be imagined now.

12 Stamford Hill Estate

Stamford Hill, N16

DATE 1931–39
ARCHITECT London County Council Architect's Department
CLIENT London County Council

The Stamford Hill Estate is a typical inter-war London County Council block dwellings estate included here for both its architectural quality and its unusually full surviving plans and documentation. It was built over an extended period in the thirties, originally planned as 277 dwellings, but eventually comprising 517 flats. It is therefore a medium-sized estate in the LCC's output, comparable with Shore Road in Hackney, Clapham Park, Streatham Hill and the Loughborough Estate in Lambeth.

The LCC chose a site on the east side of Stamford Hill (the dividing line between the former boroughs of Hackney and Stoke Newington), between Lynmouth Road and Portland Avenue. The area changed considerably during the early 20th century as large late-Georgian villas made way for settlement of a much higher density. This was a typical location for this type of development as tenants required easy access to their places of work in the City or central London. Rail and tram lines were close by. Earlier on, the LCC had misjudged the critical question of location by building estates which were too far from central London, such as the White Hart Lane Estate at Tottenham. These outlying estates proved difficult to let because people could not afford the fares into London, and the travelling took too long. The decision to proceed with the Stamford Hill scheme was taken in July 1928. Several large houses with large gardens were acquired by Compulsory Purchase Order during 1930. An area which had until then been sparsely populated was rapidly transformed to provide homes for over 1,000 people.

The scheme was developed under the 1924 Housing Act, one of several acts which on the one hand enabled and encouraged metropolitan and local authorities to provide public housing, backed by financial support from central government, and on the other hand controlled how they did it. In this particular case, this was not a slum clearance scheme, but one which was designed to augment the housing stock, providing homes 'for the working classes'. Affordable housing for rent was still in desperately short supply following the First World War. This particular Act allowed the developer (here the LCC) to receive a government subsidy of £7 10s. per dwelling for a period of 40 years, supplemented by a further contribution from local rates of 50% of the state subsidy. In return, the flats were to be let at rents fixed according to strictly controlled criteria. The shortfall which the LCC had to provide was estimated at about £15 7s. 6d. per flat per year for 40 years.

The estate was first planned to have 277 flats, each with its own bathroom and kitchen in eight blocks, mainly in buildings of five storeys with small portions in four and six storeys. The LCC Minutes of 28 October 1930 noted that 'in order to accord with the amenities of the important thoroughfare on

· SECTION A-A ·   · BACK ELEVATIC

Stamford Hill Estate.
Plan of Malvern House,
c1929

which the buildings will abut, we have given careful attention to the elevation, and we are confident that the design will give general satisfaction'. Tenders were invited from selected firms in January 1930, and Rowley Brothers of Tottenham were chosen. The building costs were estimated at £185,000.

The first flats were ready for occupation in 1931. The blocks were named after British hill ranges; Cheviot, Clent, Cotswold, Chiltern, Malvern, Laindon, Pentland and Quantock House. The architectural style is sober Neo-Georgian. Here, as in many other LCC block dwellings of the period, construction was of solid brickwork, with floors of steel and concrete finished in the living and bedrooms with boards and elsewhere with cement. Staircases were of concrete, partitions of concrete slabs, and roofs of timber with red tiles. The steep roofs have dormer windows. Windows throughout were timber sashes, with small panes in Neo-Georgian style. The central block, Malvern House, was flanked by other L- or C-shaped blocks. Distinctive touches included concrete balconies, bays, curved arches at ground floor level, square rainwater pipes and attractive patterned hoppers. The normal erection time for a typical five-storey block was nine to 12 months. These were all 'walk up' blocks without lifts and with balcony access. (Lifts were later added to Quantock House.) In 1934 the LCC designed and adopted four type plans for the internal layout of flats, which can be seen in the layout of the five blocks which were added later (Sidlaw, Brecon, Arran, Berwyn and Wicklow). Room

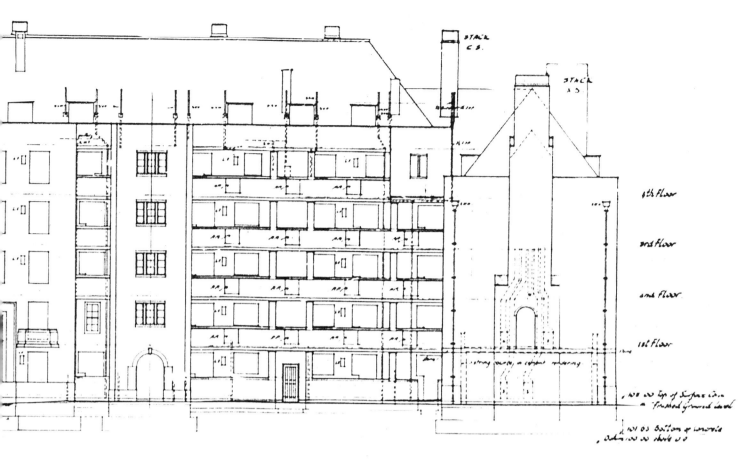

WEST WING .

heights were typically 8 ft. 6 in., and in the flats built on this estate average room areas were 160 sq. ft. in living rooms, 120 sq. ft. in first bedrooms and 100 sq. ft. in other bedrooms. Electricity was supplied, and gas was also available for cooking and heating. The LCC fixed rents (approved by the Minister of Health, but excluding rates and water) which ranged from 13s. 6d. for a 3-room ground floor flat (excluding kitchen and bathroom) to 18s. 6d. for a 5-room maisonette. Evidently there were complaints that the rents were too high, for in July 1932 the Housing Committee Minutes recorded; 'The flats on this estate … are provided to accommodate persons living and working in or near the central areas of London who are obliged to reside in reasonable proximity to their places of employment and are unable to avail themselves of accommodation at outlying cottage estates. They are not intended for the poorer class of tenants of persons displaced by the Council for whom other accommodation is specially provided. The tenants of the dwellings now in question will be put to less expense in travelling to and from their work than tenants who have to travel daily between London and outlying cottage estates.' The LCC stuck to the belief that the rents were reasonable, and that the flats were to be 'let to ordinary applicants who can afford to pay the rents of this class of accommodation'.

By May 1933 the eight blocks were complete, and the estate occupied 5¾ acres. The estate was clearly popular with tenants. Clunn's *Face of London*

(1951) noted that 'this is one of their [the LCC's] finest housing estates and so attractive are these blocks of workers' flats that many quite wealthy people have tried unsuccessfully to obtain accommodation here'. Many more applied for tenancies than were available. It was recognised that there was a shortage of larger flats, which were provided on the Stamford Hill Estate. However, it was also recognised that rents on the estate were the highest among LCC block dwelling estates. In February 1935, plans were made to enlarge the estate by building a further three blocks to the north. The following year, the adjacent Gipsy Lawn Tennis Club at the east of the site was compulsorily purchased, and two existing blocks of flats were extended and another two built. At completion, there were 517 flats on the estate in an area of approximately 11 acres. Yet, for all the LCC's zeal in building working class housing, there were few facilities such as shops, play areas or a community hall, and there was no attempt to introduce workshops or other places of employment (as had sometimes been the case before 1914).

Ownership of the estate passed to the GLC in 1965, and in turn to the London Borough of Hackney c1981 prior to the dissolution of the GLC in 1986. In a survey carried out by the council in 1995/96, the cost of refurbishment required was estimated at almost £4,000 per flat, an indication of the cumulative years of neglect of this once-grand estate. As with several other council-run estates in need of major refurbishment, the tenants have recently been consulted about who their future landlord should be: the council or a housing association. As a result, the estate will be run in future by a housing association.

London Fields Lido

London Fields, E8

DATE	1932
ARCHITECTS	possibly by H A Rowbotham and T L Smithson
CLIENT	London County Council

The idea of building a lido in this part of Hackney was first mooted in the late 1920s. Funds were available from the government as compensation for appropriating land at Hackney Marsh in 1915 to build a munitions factory. The first suggestions were to build the lido at Hackney Marsh, but the London County Council suggested London Fields as a more central location: 'this open space is more central than Hackney Marsh and is more convenient of access for the densely populated neighbourhood within the county boundary; moreover, the site of the bath … would be between the existing open-air baths under the control of the council at Victoria-park and Highbury-fields.' Hackney Borough Council was keen to take on sole management of the pool once built. However the LCC had its way, and the pool was opened on 30 April 1932 by Sir William Sidney, Chairman of the LCC's Parks and Open Spaces Committee. The construction cost of £10,000 and the running costs were split equally between the LCC and Hackney Council.

Open air bathing is a peculiarly Cockney tradition. By the early thirties, London could boast almost a dozen open air pools, whilst most provincial cities had yet to build their first. The tradition can be traced back to at least the mid-19th century, when metropolitan open spaces began to be created. These landscaped parks often included lakes, some of which were eventually regulated by the LCC as bathing places. The benefits of learning to swim – safety, health and exercise – were beginning to be recognised. One or two parks, such as Hampstead Heath, still have bathing lakes. The first open air pool in London

London Fields Lido in its heyday. view of the magnificent 50 metre pool, refreshment kiosk and cascade erator

London Fields Lido. An atmospheric winter view of the icy pool

was opened on Tooting Common in 1906. Built by the LCC, this was a pool of truly heroic dimensions: 18 lengths to a mile and a capacity in excess of a million gallons of water. In other respects, its facilities were rather basic.

During the 1920s, the LCC constructed a further six pools, at Eltham Park, Millwall Recreation Ground, Royal Victoria Gardens, Southwark Park, Highbury Fields and Peckham Rye. These were all basic, but the LCC progressively upgraded the pools, introducing experimental filtration equipment at Highbury Fields and Peckham Rye by 1927. By the end of the Twenties, the LCC had a defined policy for the construction of open air swimming pools. Any local council interested in a pool could approach the LCC who, if in agreement, would provide the site, pay for the construction and contribute half the running costs. This period also saw the widespread introduction of mixed bathing sessions for which a charge was normally made. This meant that open air bathing finally shrugged off its ascetic macho image and became an accepted family pastime with a resulting increase in its popularity. Against this background, the lido at London Fields was built.

Architecturally the London Fields Lido formed a pair with the pool opened the previous year in Kennington Park; they were quite different from what had gone before, and represented a new approach to pool design which was to be replicated in various forms all over the country in the years prior to the Second World War. These pools were equipped with substantial well-designed buildings housing modern filtration equipment, ample changing areas for individuals and groups, a first aid room and a refreshment kiosk. Both lidos consisted of a brick enclosure with a symmetrical series of pitched roof pavilions. The most substantial range of buildings was at the southern end and housed the turnstiles, filtration equipment and staff quarters. The changing areas were provided in two identical ranges along the eastern and western sides, each with a central brick pavilion connected to each end of the pool by arcades of wooden individual changing cubicles. The north end was given over as a sun-bathing terrace and the only other buildings consisted of a free standing flat-roofed refreshment kiosk (not provided at Kennington Park) situated behind a green tiled cascade aerator.

The 165 by 66 ft. pool ranges in depth from 2 ft. 6 in. to 7 ft. 6 in. and has a capacity of 350,000 gallons. This was the only LCC pool to be closed for the entire duration of the Second World War and reopened, after extensive restoration, in 1951. The abolition of the GLC in 1986 was catastrophic for London's lidos, with few lasting more than a season or two under the control of cash-starved local boroughs. Only three out of 13 are still operating – Tooting, Brockwell Park in Lambeth, and Parliament Hill, Hampstead. London Fields Lido has been disused since the 1988 season, but a group of local residents is exploring ways of reopening it. With the current spate of warm summers, it would surely be popular and successful, and it would be the only 50 metre pool in the area.

14 Manor House Underground Station

Green Lanes/Seven Sisters Road, N4

DATE   1932
ARCHITECT   Charles Holden
CLIENT   London Electric Railway Co

anor House Underground Station.
oking Hall, November 1932

The Piccadilly line first opened on 15 December 1906, running from Finsbury Park to Hammersmith. During the inter-war period, there was an ever increasing demand for more and better railway services in London. The task of developing and constructing new lines continued although the services were still privately owned. There was hot political debate about how to deliver improvements to the system and at the same time steps were taken

towards the unification of London's transport system. By the mid-1920s the Ministry of Transport had become concerned about travelling facilities in north and north east London and as a result of their official investigations, an extension to the Piccadilly line was proposed to alleviate the problem of heavy traffic. One major side benefit of such a large construction project was the employment it provided.

The Piccadilly line was extended north from Finsbury Park to Cockfosters (then a rural hamlet), and west to Uxbridge in 1930-33. These extensions resulted in a 32 mile tube line, then the longest on electrified tracks in London. The stations on the new section were designed during one of most celebrated periods in London's transport history when the illustrious duo of Frank Pick, managing director of London Underground Railways, and Charles Holden, architect, forged a complete corporate identity for transport in London, striving for good quality and unified designs. Some of Holden's most outstanding stations are further north on the Piccadilly line, at Southgate and Arnos Grove.

The section from Finsbury Park to Arnos Grove opened on 19 September 1932. Manor House was the first station on the northern extension of the line beyond Finsbury Park, and was built below ground at the intersection of Seven Sisters Road and Green Lanes. Nine stairways led down to the ticket hall and escalators to platform level. The platforms were wider than usual to cope with extra passengers. Originally there was a waiting shelter on Green Lanes and a tram station, with two tram shelters in Seven Sisters Road to allow for interchange between tram and tube train under cover. After the introduction of trolley buses in 1939, the tram shelters fell into disuse and were removed in 1951. There was also a distinctive illuminated road direction sign designed by Holden in the middle of the junction.

The ticket hall was designed with an efficient flow of passengers in mind. The plan was asymmetrical, and any dead areas were used for kiosks and offices. The ceiling was decorated with a pattern of circular mouldings which fitted the unusual shape. The tunnels at Manor House, Turnpike Lane and Wood Green were lined to give an elliptical profile and furniture and equipment were recessed into the tunnel walls to maintain the clean lines. Tiles were biscuit cream and bright blue. Ventilation grilles in the platform walls were designed by Harold Stabler and show idealised visions evoked by the locality.

Manor House is the only tube station in the borough of Hackney, an area poorly served by underground lines. Now in a poor state of repair, it would benefit from major refurbishment to bring it up to the standard of other recently renovated stations on the Piccadilly line.

15 Evelyn Court

Amhurst Road, E8

DATE	1933–34
ARCHITECTS	Burnet, Tait & Lorne
CLIENT	Four Per Cent Industrial Dwellings Company Ltd

Evelyn Court was built by the Four Per Cent Industrial Dwellings Company Ltd, founded in 1885 as a semi-philanthropic company to 'provide the industrial classes with more commodious and healthy lodgings and dwellings … giving them the maximum accommodation at a minimum rent'. It was one of several housing associations founded in the second half of the 19th century to tackle the problems caused by poor housing in the East End, especially around Whitechapel and Spitalfields. Slum properties were being demolished but not replaced, so there was a net reduction in the amount of cheap housing available for rent. Waves of Jewish immigrants fleeing the pogroms of eastern Europe arrived in London in the early 1880s, swelling the numbers requiring housing. The United Synagogue was particularly concerned about living conditions amongst the Jewish poor, and formed a commission which investigated conditions in the East End, reporting in January 1885.

They proposed that to achieve lower rents, returns to shareholders might be restricted to 4%, instead of a more usual 7 to 8% typically achievable from other blocks of model dwellings. Thus the Four Per Cent was founded and held its first meeting on 1 July 1885; Sir Nathaniel (later Lord) Rothschild was a founder director, with other board members – many of whom already had an interest in working class housing – drawn from the Anglo-Jewish bourgeoisie. Although the society was founded by Jews who were concerned about their co-religionists, occupation of the tenements they built was not limited to Jews.

The first tenements built were Rothschild Buildings at Flower and Dean Street, Spitalfields, completed in 1887 (now demolished). These were immediately popular and over-subscribed. Architecturally the first buildings were rather grim and utilitarian, but although interior layouts were very basic, the designs were ahead of their time with self-contained kitchen and washing facilities

Evelyn Court. View from the roof of one of the blocks, looking towards the north-west corner of the site. Photograph from *The Architect & Building News*, February 1935

for each flat. Further schemes followed in the East End, and then at Stoke Newington (Coronation and Imperial Avenues off Victorian Road, 1903), and in Hackney (the stylish Art Nouveau Navarino Mansions, 1903-04). The company's name changed to the present Industrial Dwellings Society (1885) Ltd in 1951.

Evelyn Court was the company's next project after Navarino Mansions. Because a 4% return was still required for shareholders, the company felt compelled to explore more economical methods of building turning to a model scheme developed by the builders Holland, Hannen & Cubitt with the architect Francis Lorne. Evelyn Court was constructionally innovative for its date, when most public housing in Britain was still being built from traditional load-bearing masonry. Instead, a reinforced concrete frame was used, with reinforced concrete floors and walls of reinforced concrete and brick. Use of repetitive forms and techniques in the construction process helped achieve considerable savings in building costs. As *The Architect & Building News* reported, the flats 'represent one of the most interesting and largest attempts to provide up-to-date housing on an economic basis without resorting to a subsidy'. The scheme was a bold and moderately successful attempt to move away from the style of tenement estates of the type built by the London County Council at the time. Gone were the traditional materials, the sash windows, the quirky detailing and the access balconies. In their place came concrete standardisation.

Built on a long rectangular site to the east of Amhurst Road sloping towards Hackney Downs, the estate consists of 10 austere five-storey blocks mostly arranged in an unimaginative 'toast rack' plan and containing 160 two-bedroom and 160 three-bedroom flats. In addition, drying rooms, cycle/pram sheds, a caretaker's cottage, workshop and office and two children's playrooms were provided. Francis Lorne was closely involved throughout the scheme and accompanied the Prince of Wales around the construction site in 1934. He was much concerned at the time with the establishment of a new systematic methodology in building, and instigated the publication through the Architectural Press of *The Information Book* which remained a standard work of reference for architects well into the sixties.

Each staircase serves two flats on each floor. Each flat consists of two 11 ft. 9 in. wide bays, each subdivided in depth to yield a total of four rooms, with an extra room for the larger flats squeezed out of the rear of the 8 ft. 1 in. wide stairwell. Consideration was given to standardising the processes of shuttering and reinforcement in order to economise as much as possible. Insulation boards were used for shuttering the floors and left in situ, forming the ceiling of the flat below. This provided both heat and sound insulation. Remaining walls were brick infill and the exterior was originally rendered in white, with green staircase towers, rising from a brick plinth. Central to the building method was a temporary on-site concrete mixing and pumping plant which was able to deliver 20 cubic yards of liquid concrete per hour to anywhere in the construction area.

Over 60 years since its completion, Evelyn Court still stands out as an unusual, highly disciplined project, though the construction methods used have never been as generally popular as Francis Lorne had hoped.

The German Hospital, East Wing

Fassett Square, E8

DATE   1935-36
ARCHITECT   Thomas Tait (of Burnet, Tait & Lorne)
CLIENT   The German Hospital

The German Hospital, East
Wing facing onto Fassett
Square. Photograph from
The Architect & Building
News, 1936

Thomas Tait's (1882-1954) potent combination of outstanding technical and stylistic ability produced some of Britain's most successful inter-war hospital buildings. These include the Royal Masonic Hospital, Ravenscourt Park (1930-33). As the new wing at the German Hospital was an extension to an existing range of buildings, the architect was freed from certain formal constraints, and the design of the new wing was largely determined by the various functions contained within it.

A bequest from a former Swiss patient, Mrs B Rienaccher, enabled the hospital to purchase neighbouring land in Fassett Square. The new wing was opened on 10 July 1936, and is the most architecturally distinguished building in the entire group. The ground and first floors were for private patients' rooms. The second floor contained nurses' accommodation. The third floor housed the maternity unit which consisted of individual rooms, a five bed ward, a nursery and the cantilevered delivery unit which forms a prominent feature on the north façade. The fourth floor was the children's ward with a flexible arrangement of glazed screens so that the sister could command a view of the entire floor. This floor also had a continuous sun balcony along the western elevation onto which beds could be wheeled. The roof was laid out as a terrace and garden for convalescents. In many respects the building was at the forefront of medical and architectural thinking of the time.

The building has a steel frame and is L-shaped. It is faced with yellow sand-lime bricks, highlighted by wide-grouted blue tiles on the piers between the top floor windows and around the doorways onto the rounded sun-balconies on each floor. The bricks are laid in a bond of two stretchers to one header, a favourite device in Burnet, Tait & Lorne's work. The entrance front is dominated by the massive concrete canopy above the doorway. Internally, the building provided a bright, spacious and hygienic environment. Corners and crevices were avoided, and hard, easy-to-clean

surfaces used. The lower portion of the corridor walls were tiled in primrose coloured Janus tiles from Germany which were continued as architraving over the door openings. Internal doors were blue with chrome fittings. Floors were terrazzo in the corridors and bathrooms, and lino in the wards (painted cream) curving upwards to the walls for easy cleaning. This is a recurring theme throughout the building – the join in walling materials was made flush by a metal strip, basins in the rooms stood proud of the walls, and the windows could be cleaned from the inside. The architect felt that his treatment of the staircases worked particularly well.

The greatest influence on the new wing at the German Hospital was the Tuberculosis Sanitorium at Paimio in Finland (1928-33) by Alvar Aalto. Undoubtedly it was from this building that the ideas of a roof garden and the disposition of the wards in relation to the balconies were derived. The children's ward apart, all floors have a streamlined sun-balcony at the south-west corner in line with the current medical thinking that patients should mix in small groups for convalescence rather than be confined in isolation. There are clear influences from recent Dutch architecture, attributable to Tait's interest in the work of W M Dudok. The reviewer in *The Architect & Building News* of 30 October 1936 wrote: 'Every thing is flush and suave and well finished, conveying the impression that even the slightest detail has been considered in the round and in relation to every other part and to the whole'. In summary, the design and detailing and their execution mark the building out as being in the forefront of modern design in 1930s Britain.

The German Hospital was closed in 1987 following rationalisation of the National Health Service. Many of the buildings have been converted into social housing, whilst the East Wing is being developed as private apartments.

For further information on the history of the hospital, see Elizabeth McKellar, *The German Hospital Hackney. A social and architectural history, 1845-1987*, The Hackney Society, 1991.

17 Hackney Town Hall and Municipal Offices

Mare Street, E8

DATE   1934-37
ARCHITECTS   Lanchester & Lodge
CLIENT   Hackney Borough Council

Hackney Town Hall. The new building is almost complete, whilst the old one is being demolished to make way for gardens, 1937. The flank wall of the Hackney Empire Theatre is on the right

A huge number of town halls were constructed during the 1930s in response to the vastly increased responsibilities of local government in the inter-war period. In Hackney's case, the council considered enlarging the 1866 town hall, but decided that a new one was required. A limited competition was held, and the architects selected were Lanchester & Lodge. The old Victorian building was demolished, the new one erected further back from Mare Street, and formal gardens including a war memorial were laid out in front.

...ackney Town Hall. The foundation
...one was laid on 23 October 1934 by
...r Edward Hilton Young, Minister
... Health, with the Mayor, Cllr. C.
...sher Yates JP, looking on

The generous site allowed for a spacious, square building on a traditional courtyard plan. Each side has its own entrance and space for vehicles to draw up directly outside, unlike its Victorian predecessor. In contrast with that building, the new one is in a conventional Art Deco style. The building is four storeys high, faced on all sides in Portland stone.

Although the internal plan is traditional, it is logical and very complete, with a grand entrance hall and staircase leading up to the council chamber on the first floor. The ground floor was used for offices for the departments of the Borough Engineer, Medical Officer, Treasurer, and Registrar of Births, Deaths and Marriages. Committee rooms, the Mayor's Parlour, and the Town Clerk's office are ranged along the front at first floor level. The first floor also contains a handsome suite of Assembly Rooms on the west side – all at double height. The interiors are well-preserved, with specially designed light fittings and furniture. The top floor houses staff quarters and the caretaker's flat whilst the basement is given over to storage and plant rooms.

In addition to the well-designed setting, the Council Chamber, upper hall, and committee rooms have an undeniable grandeur and are enhanced by superbly opulent Art Deco light fittings. The stream-lined lamps mounted on truncated pillars on the main staircase are particularly distinctive. Furniture for the principal rooms was designed by Waring & Gillow, one of the leading firms of the day.

Lanchester (1863-1953) designed many other public buildings including Deptford Town Hall (1900–03) and the Central Hall, Westminster (1905-11). After forming a partnership with Lodge in 1923, they went on to design a number of other civic buildings including Beckenham Town Hall (1932, now demolished).

After the amalgamation of the three metropolitan boroughs, Hackney, Shoreditch and Stoke Newington, to form the London Borough of Hackney in 1965, Hackney Town Hall retained its function, whilst Shoreditch and Stoke Newington found other uses.

18 Lennox House

Cresset Road, E9

DATE   1937
ARCHITECT   J E M MacGregor
CLIENT   The Bethnal Green and East London Housing Association

This ziggurat design is one of the most remarkable housing schemes in Hackney. The original idea was that the central portion of the building beneath the stepped flats should be used as a covered market, the income from which was to subsidise the rents of the flats above. However, during the building period, land in the area was designated for residential use only, so the economic plans for the building were undermined. During the war, the space was rented by the local council and used as a store for air raid precaution equipment, and a decontamination centre. The density is 75 dwellings to the acre, in contrast to the London County Council's preferred 30.

The ziggurat design with private balconies was an unusual solution to flatted housing. The housing association was committed to providing a garden for

Lennox House. Photograph from *The Architect & Building News*, June 1942

each flat (except those on the ground floor). Each balcony is accessed from the living room of the flat. The flats are mostly arranged in pairs, and are reached by three sets of external stairways. The recesses for these stairs separate the balconies from each other, providing privacy. Generous window space and the step-back section resulted in light interiors. The inspiration for the step-back can be traced to a 1925 apartment block for working class tenants in the Rue des Amiraux in Paris by Henri Sauvage. The Brunswick Centre in Bloomsbury is an example of a later development using the same technique.

The construction of Lennox House is an innovative reinforced concrete frame with hollow-tile floors. It survived two bombs which fell close by during the Second World War. The 11-inch hollow brick walls are supported separately at each floor and the floor slabs are expressed in the exterior elevation. The use of a 'cosy' stove in each living room, which also incorporated a vent through to heat the bedroom, was an important and popular addition. The chimneys for these stoves slope inwards as they travel up the building, one from each side: they form a triangle meeting on the top floor and emerging vertically through the roof. There are 35 flats on five storeys arranged with three-bedroom flats on the first floor, one-bedroom flats on the top floor and two-bedroom flats elsewhere. The hipped roof and Neo-Georgian flavour perhaps detract from a more modern style.

The architect John MacGregor (1890-1984) was fascinated by engineering and its application to architecture. Much of his work was concerned with the repair of historic buildings including castles, stately homes and churches, and he was closely involved with the work of the Society for the Protection of Ancient Buildings. In his own building designs he often combined the use of new materials, such as reinforced concrete, with traditional elements, such as steep pitched tile roofs and brickwork. For example, in cottages in Ongar, Essex, built in 1936, he used an exposed concrete frame resembling a traditional Tudor design. His interest in using modern materials inexpensively led to his involvement in the development of low cost, precast concrete housing prototypes, collaborating with the British Cast Concrete Federation. He was also interested in transport and urban planning, and particularly with their impact on historic town centres.

Lennox House may well be his most successful building, but has gone largely unnoticed in the architectural press. MacGregor expressed his aim as being 'a building composed of many separate homes, each having as much fresh air and light as possible, and a real substitute for the garden or yard … together with a sense of privacy'.

Axonometric drawing of Lennox House

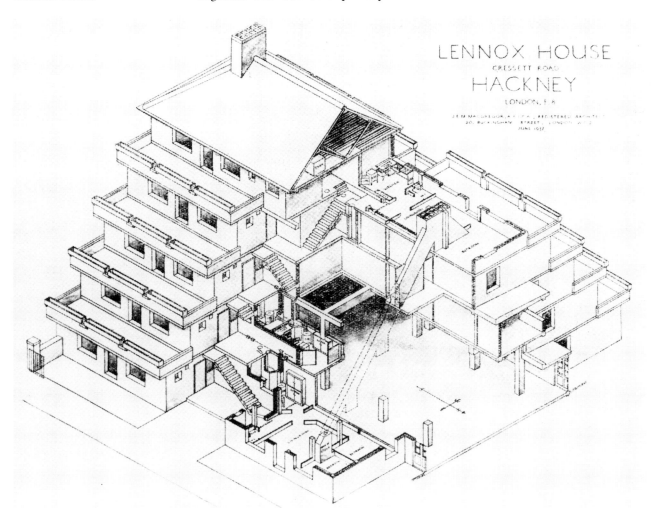

LENNOX HOUSE
CRESSETT ROAD
HACKNEY
LONDON, E.8

The Rio Cinema

107 Kingsland High Street, Dalston, E8

DATE   1937
ARCHITECT   Frederick E Bromige
CLIENT   Capital and Provincial News Theatres

opposite The Rio Cinema. 1998

The Rio Cinema is a rare survivor from a period when Hackney had many more cinemas than today. It began life as an auctioneer's shop, but in 1909 the architect W E Trent converted it into a 175-seat electric picture house for its owner, Clara Ludski. The venture appears to have been a success, as in 1913 the two neighbouring properties were purchased, and the renowned cinema architects, Adams & Coles of Hackney, were asked to convert the premises into a proper cinema.

They created a tall, rich, elaborate design. A high, steep balcony was installed. Underneath this was a double-height tearoom set in a Diocletian arch with windows overlooking Kingsland High Street. The fronts to the balconies were lavishly decorated, and a pair of Ionic columns guarded the proscenium arch. The new cinema, which opened in 1915 as the Kingsland Empire, seated 956 people, with a further 174 standing places. In 1920 a pipe organ was installed, and in 1929 sound equipment was installed into the projection box.

In 1937 the interior was remodelled again after an inspection by the London County Council found the ventilation sub-standard, and the waiting area too small. The architect F E Bromige gutted the interior just leaving the walls and roof, and installed a lower auditorium, new circle, new waiting areas, a foyer, operating box and plenum chamber in the shell. An advert in the *Hackney Gazette* on 1 December 1937 announced the opening of the new cinema early that month, 'presenting a modern super in miniature ... with all the latest ultra modern improvements'. The *Ideal Kinema* reported that the interior was decorated 'in a modern style with sweeping lines, and the colouring is in a grey-blue and warm brown, and the seating a dark red, which is set off by red festoon tabs'. On the Kingsland Road elevation, a neon sign with letters over three metres high gave the cinema's new name – Classic. The foyer is topped by a distinctive drum, with a fluted façade above. In fact, the remodelled cinema seated just 561 people, considerably fewer than previously. Ironically this may have helped the cinema to survive several decades of low cinema attendance. The building is a typically curvaceous example of Bromige's cinema work, and retains its complete Art Deco interior of 1937. It is the only one of his four surviving cinemas still in undivided cinema use.

The Classic remained in business as a repertory cinema until the 1950s. It then went through a number of changes as the Classic Cartoon Cinema in the Fifties, the Tatler Cinema Club in the Seventies, eventually becoming the Rio in 1976. The only alteration to Bromige's 1937 design is the addition of the cafe to one side. The recent refurbishment programme at the Rio has given one of the few cinemas in the borough a new lease of life.

Stoke Newington Civic Centre

Stoke Newington Church Street, N16

DATE   1935-37
ARCHITECT   J Reginald Truelove
CLIENT   Stoke Newington Borough Council

Stoke Newington Town Hall. The Council Chamber. Photograph from *The Architect & Building News*, October 1937

The Civic Centre comprises the Town Hall, Assembly Hall and Reference Library. They were built on the site of an early 18th century terrace, which had replaced the Manor House of Stoke Newington. Before this building existed, the Council had used a vestry hall in Milton Grove. This complex of buildings is adjacent to the earlier library building in Stoke Newington Church Street. The Assembly Hall faces onto Church Street, with a large recessed stone portico forming the entrance. The Town Hall follows this line, then curves away from Church Street, with a recessed stone entrance with large bronze doors on the curved façade. This façade faces the Old St. Mary's churchyard and Clissold Park, and returns along the line of Lordship Terrace to the rear where car parks and the business entrance are located. The overall style is quite conservative for the date.

The architect J Reginald Truelove (1887-1942) was much involved with architecture for the military and worked extensively with the War Graves Commission after the First World War. One of his most successful designs is the Memorial to the Missing at Vis-en-Artois near Arras in northern France.

The podium is of Portland stone with brickwork above and stone dressings. The handmade bricks are long and thin, the bricklaying of excellent quality. The lines and features of the design are simple. The openings for windows and entrances are emphasised by deep reveals. The windows are of steel, with elegant margin lights. At first floor level the Council Chamber with domed roof and barrel-vaulted galleries, panelled in Australian walnut, forms the central space. Committee rooms, the Mayor's Parlour and other official function rooms are situated around the curved façade. These are reached via a grand teak staircase with a balustrade in wrought iron and silvered bronze. Two light wells either side of the Council Chamber allow light into the deep plan. Below on the ground floor are the usual offices for rates, clerks, etc accessed from Lordship Terrace. The Assembly Hall is rectangular with a gallery on the south (Church Street) side, and stage with proscenium arch. The sprung dance floor is of Canadian maple. As remarkable as the details of its plan and construction is the fact that the Civic Centre still retains its wartime camouflage, swirls of faded paint-work covering its façade like wave patterns on a beach.

This is a handsome suite of buildings, built to a high quality, and reflecting the considerable civic pride at the time. The quality of construction has no doubt helped the buildings to survive. Unfortunately, the buildings are no longer in prime condition. The once-magnificent Council Chamber has had a false ceiling inserted, obscuring the dome, and is now unsympathetically used as offices. It would be more appropriate kept as a fine civic room. The superb walnut furniture it once contained has disappeared. Small offices have been knocked through to make larger ones, thereby ruining the original plan. However, many of the excellent features such as the parquet flooring and brass window fittings survive, and should be preserved and enhanced. External railings have recently been restored. During building, a panel of brickwork from the original manor house (about 1 metre square) was incorporated into the exterior west wall of the Assembly Hall.

Stoke Newington Town Hall. The Lord Mayor of London receiving councillors at the opening ceremony on 28 September 1937

21 # Bankstock Buildings

42-44 De Beauvoir Crescent, N1

DATE 1938-39
ARCHITECT Robert Sharp
CLIENT Commercial Structures Ltd

This sizeable factory was built in 1938-39 on the site of Victorian terraced houses in De Beauvoir Crescent. The building is five storeys high, and backs on to the Regent's Canal, adjacent to the Whitmore Bridge over the canal. When the factory was built, the rest of De Beauvoir Crescent contained semi-detached villas, but these have not survived post-war redevelopment. Perhaps the proximity to the canal and Kingsland Basin was an important factor in locating the factory here. It was designed by Robert Sharp for

Bankstock Buildings, 1998

Commercial Structures Ltd of Leyton, building contractors and engineers specialising in reinforced concrete.

Reinforced concrete pillars with cantilevered arms support wide-span floors. The exterior is of stock brick, with bands of yellow faience tiles. The windows are by Crittall. The building is rectangular with a semi-circular projecting tower feature at the north-west corner. This tower gives the building a distinctive Thirties feel, and makes it noticeable in an area which was much redeveloped in the post-war period. In fact, the tower contains staircases, leaving the interior floors as uninterrupted spaces for manufacturing. Just the ground floor has remained as an undivided space, and is the only floor where the unusually-shaped concrete pillars can still be clearly seen.

The building seems to have been a speculative venture by Commercial Structures Ltd. The large, open floors of the building were designated as 'manufacturing space' in Sharp's plans. On completion, the first occupiers were Carreras Ltd of Hampstead, manufacturers of tobacco and cigarettes, famous for their black cat trademark. From 1952, the building was used by printers, and it is now in mixed use – light industrial, live/work units and offices. An additional floor in a very unsympathetic style was added in the late 1980s.

The architect Robert Sharp (1881-1950) worked in Aberdeen, India and London. In England he developed a reputation for designing motor garages during the 1920s, which was quite a new building type at that time. His work includes the OK Sauce Factory at Southfields, and four London motor garages; the best-known of these is the stylish Blue Bird Garage at 350 King's Road, Chelsea (1924, converted in 1997 into the Conran-owned Bluebird Restaurant). This was said to be the largest garage in Europe when it was built. Other motor garages he designed are Moon's Garage in Kensington (1932, now demolished), the Lex Garage at the corner of Lexington Street and Brewer Street, Soho (1929, now altered) and another Lex Garage in Wellington Road, St. John's Wood (also altered). His buildings were enthusiastically reviewed by contemporary writers; *The Architect & Building News* wrote of Moon's, 'it is easily the best-looking garage in London'. The way Sharp handles large spaces, using the latest concrete technology, is the obvious link between his garages and this factory building. In a modest way, this block is Hackney's answer to the famous 1930s factories of the Great West Road.

Brett Manor

Brett Road, E8

DATE	1947–48
ARCHITECT	Edward Mills
CLIENT	Manor Charitable Trustees

This modest block of flats in an obscure back road has claims to be the most important building of the post-war period in Hackney. Not only was this the first reinforced concrete box frame building to be completed in London, but it also established a series of stylistic motifs that have become indelibly linked with this form of construction. Brett Manor was built as low cost flats for the Manor Charitable Trustees, to provide affordable rented housing for ex-servicemen, old members of the Eton Manor Boys' Club, Hackney, or war widows of old members.

The site is small and awkward, with roads on three sides. It is situated just west of the Narroway (Mare Street). Part of the site had been used for

Brett Manor, the western elevation. Photograph from *Architectural Design*, November 1951

underground air raid shelters during the war, leaving very deep basements.

In the immediate post-war era all privately constructed housing was subject to stringent price controls. For flats, the Ministry of Health limit was £1,500 per unit of 950 square ft. – a sum which required the architect to cost-cut at every turn and make full use of his ingenuity to make the most of a limited budget. Here a further allowance was made for demolishing the air raid shelters and dealing with the deeper than normal foundations.

Mills designed Brett Manor as a single five storey block of nine flats – eight maisonettes and a penthouse with roof garden. The eight maisonettes are each one structural bay wide and two floors high. The living rooms are on one floor, the bedrooms on the other. There is a single staircase block, and gallery access on the second floor. This inspired response to the dictates of a rigid framework meant that only one true access gallery was required. Each flat has a full width balcony on the west elevation and the ground floor flats also have access to individual gardens.

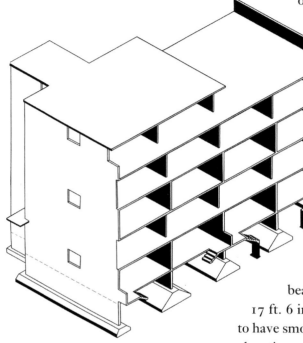

Axonometric drawing of Brett Manor showing the box frame structure

The structural system was devised in conjunction with the engineers Ove Arup & Partners and represents a development of the ideas which Ove Arup had developed in the 1930s, principally at Highpoint I in Highgate (1933-35). The reinforced concrete box is the frame, having its own inherent structural strength akin to an egg box. It consists of continuous 6 in. reinforced concrete slabs and 6 in. load bearing spine walls acting as the dividers between flats. Each flat is 17 ft. 6 in. wide. Beams and columns were not needed, so it was possible to have smooth, flush wall finishes. Non-structural walls on the east and west elevations are brick cavity. Mills left the box frame exposed on alternate floors, emphasising the cellular nature of the structure and also the passive role played by the non-structural brick infilling. Significantly, it also meant that the building's structure was used as the dominant decorative element. There is a certain irony here, as one of the advantages of box-frame construction is that the structure is internalised, freeing the elevations for imaginative and decorative treatment! The structural principles used at Brett Manor were applied on a larger scale at the Spa Green Estate in Islington, completed two years later. There Arup & Partners teamed up with Berthold Lubetkin, as Arup personally had done at Highpoint I and II.

Edward Mills (1915-98) embraced many of the ideals of the modern movement in the 1930s, working with Maxwell Fry and Walter Gropius. His own practice flourished in the post-war period, and he designed schools, housing, factories and churches in Britain and abroad. His best-known building is the National Exhibition Centre near Birmingham. His writings include *The Modern Factory* (1951 and 1959) and *The Modern Church* (1956).

23 Somerford Estate

Shacklewell Road, N16

DATE   1946-49
ARCHITECT   Frederick Gibberd with G L Downing, Borough Engineer
CLIENT   Hackney Borough Council

The Somerford Estate in Shacklewell Road is the most notable work in Hackney of Frederick Gibberd (1908-84), best known as the master planner of Harlow New Town, Essex and the Catholic Cathedral in Liverpool. It was designed in 1945, but not built until 1946-49. The estate embodied Gibberd's desire to combine architecture, town planning and landscape architecture, and looks at design as an enclosure of space rather than an arrangement of mass – a particular concern of the design world at that time. In an article on the three-dimensional aspects of housing layouts written in 1948, he

Somerford Estate c1948

explained 'the space we make is of great significance. It is itself intangible, but nevertheless it is quite real. You cannot feel or touch it, but once you relate objects to each other, you are conscious of the space between them'. The Somerford Estate was planned on this basis, and is significant as it predates his work at Harlow.

The estate is the first example of a mixed development in housing in England. It juxtaposes five different forms of dwelling of different heights from one to three storeys: direct access flats, gallery access flats, flatted houses, bungalows and terraced houses – a total of 150 dwellings. The layout of the whole estate ensured that a variety of forms and a range of materials, colours and textures were visible simultaneously, giving the eye relief and stimulation. This was a reaction against the monotony of Victorian terraced housing then regarded as slums. A through-road was closed in the redevelopment enabling a pattern of linked courts or closes to be laid out. The Somerford Estate was described as one of the best types of mixed development in the London area, and was given an award during the 1951 Festival of Britain. This is commemorated by a blue ceramic plaque on one of the buildings at the junction of Somerford Grove and Shacklewell Road. (The Festival of Britain plaque was designed by Abram Games [1914-96]. Educated at the Grocers' Company School, Hackney, he became one of the foremost British graphic designers of the 20th century.)

Gibberd described mixed development as 'planning the complete area as a whole series of pictures with variety in each, and unity within the whole'. He prepared a detailed survey of the site, drawing thumb-nail sketches showing both existing and proposed buildings. Consideration was given to aesthetic and social factors: the proportion of old people's bungalows to terraced housing and flats, the inclusion of communal facilities such as a chapel, laundry, branch library, public house, club room, nursery, cycle stores, garages, children's playground and a public garden. Until this time, shared services had only been made available in middle class dwellings of the 1930s and 40s. Gibberd had designed some of these, including Pullman Court, Streatham (1933-35), Park Court, Crystal Palace (1936) and Ellington Court, Southgate (1937).

Festival of Britain plaque awarded to the Somerford Estate, 1951

The different sizes of dwellings were to ensure a mixed community, and it was intended that as people's circumstances changed from single person households, to couples, to families and into old age, they would move from one size of dwelling to another according to their needs. In practice, people were not keen to move as they became attached to one house or flat, and often there was no appropriate size of dwelling when it was needed.

Gibberd designed several other mixed development housing projects in Hackney: The Beckers, Rectory Road, N16 (1958); the Beecholme Estate at Prout Road, Clapton; Kingsgate Estate at Tottenham Road, N1 (1958-61) and Parkside, Victoria Park Road in south Hackney (1964).

Woodberry Down Estate

Manor House, N4

DATE	1946–52
ARCHITECT	London County Council, based on plans by the council's former architect J H Forshaw
CLIENT	London County Council

Woodberry Down, one of the largest post-war London County Council estates, was conceived in 1936. The triangular site is roughly 44.75 acres, its boundaries formed by the New River on two sides and Green Lanes on the third. Two reservoirs to the south make this an area of natural amenity. The typical housing stock of this area was large detached Victorian villas until the land was compulsorily purchased from 1938 onwards. The scheme to redevelop Woodberry Down was extremely unpopular and attracted much criticism in the local press. The *North London Recorder*, 28 November 1938, described it as 'the LCC's gigantic scheme of rehousing the slum dwellers of North London

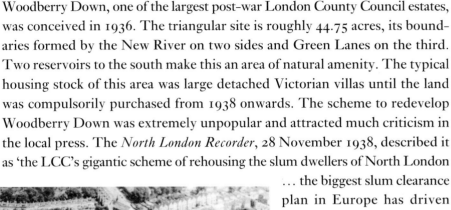

… rial view of Woodberry Down
… king south east, *c*1957. The
… ew River is on the left, the
… aight road is Seven Sisters
… ad and the East Reservoir at
… e top right

… the biggest slum clearance plan in Europe has driven away people whose families have lived in Stoke Newington for generations. Morrison has driven them out of London. They can find no homes to suit them in the area under his rule. In their place come people who will make Morrison even more secure in his County Hall office.' (Herbert Morrison was Leader of the LCC from 1934-40; Labour had won control of the council for the first time in 1934. He was Mayor of Hackney from 1920-21 and subsequently MP for South Hackney in 1923-24, 1929-31 and 1935-45.)

The scheme planned in 1938 was for a mixed development of four and five-storey blocks of flats and two-storey cottages. The blocks of flats were to be regularly spaced, parallel, and oriented north–south to give east–west light. However, the war delayed the start of the project, and when the scheme was revived in 1942 it was used as a test-bed for a number of new ideas. Most significantly, high-rise (i.e. eight-storey) blocks appeared in the mixture early in 1943; when built, these were to be the highest LCC flats in London to date, exceeding the 80 ft. zone height which had applied until then. At this time, the architect stated that the 'blocks have been carefully sited to give variety and interest to the general layout of the estate' – a much reiterated phrase. An LCC meeting in March 1943 noted, 'consideration was given to the appropriateness of this type of block to working-class tenants with families. The view was taken that the provision of lifts without attendants (as was proposed) would mean that children would have to go up by the stairs and consequently that the higher floors would be quite unattractive to tenants with families.' Even in the early 1940s, there was considerable controversy about housing families with children in high-rise blocks, and also concern about the higher cost of building them. Stoke Newington Borough Council were unhappy about the high-rise blocks, but positive aspects of 'variety and interest' were repeatedly stressed. In keeping with the mood of the time, schools, community centre and shops, etc were included in the plan – all the basic amenities of a post-war neighbourhood.

Altogether the scheme provided 1,765 dwellings to house about 6,350 people. Needwood House, the first eight-storey block to be completed, was opened on 17 February 1949. All the blocks were originally intended to be of steel frame construction faced in brick. But construction was delayed until after the war, and in the post-war period shortages of steel and bricks meant that the eight-storey blocks were built in monolithic concrete instead. Every effort was made to recycle materials in short supply – steel for the filler floors came from cut up Anderson shelters and early fencing was made from cut up ARP stretchers. Electric lifts were provided in these blocks, another innovation for their time. Flats were heated by central heating, with radiators in the living room and largest bedroom. Electric fires were also installed in the living room and first bedroom; kitchens were fitted for a gas or electric cooker.

This project, along with much of the LCC's work in the 1940s, attracted great criticism in the contemporary architectural profession. An exhibition of the LCC's work at County Hall in May 1949, and a radio broadcast by J M Richards criticising the work of the LCC stimulated a debate in the *Architects' Journal*. Criticism was received such as 'layouts are dull, architecture is unimaginative, and detailing coarse': reactions which can still be easily appreciated today. There was very little praise for the in-house LCC team, and much credit was given to private practices used by the LCC which were producing more visionary architecture, such as the Wilton Estate discussed below (see p. 73).

But despite the criticism Woodberry Down received, it represents a step towards solving the massive housing shortage of the 1930s and 1940s. It has proved popular with many tenants who are now working with the council in exploring ways to improve the estate.

Benthal Schools

Benthal Road, Stoke Newington, N16

DATE 1947–49/1966–67
ARCHITECTS London County Council Architect's Department (1947 building)
Greater London Council Architect's Department (Paul Maas)
(1966 building)
CLIENT London County Council/Inner London Education Authority

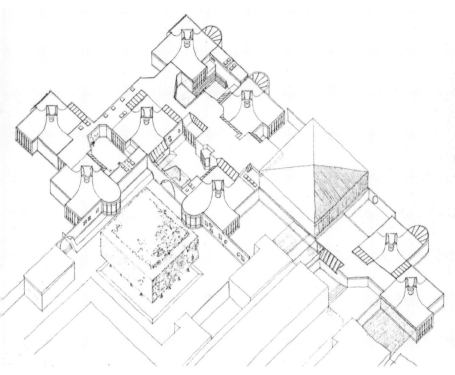

[...]nthal Primary School, bird's eye
[...]w of the 1966 building

[...]efabricated fins of the infant
[...]ssrooms being erected, 1966

With the construction of the Great Eastern Railway, the area north of Hackney Downs changed rapidly during the 1870s when it was developed with terraced housing. Until then, this area of Stoke Newington had been largely rural in character, with country houses and nursery gardens. In the middle of the area the Rendlesham Road Board School for infants was built in 1876, and adjacent to this, a substantial three-decker building for juniors was opened in 1887. The schools were built on the site of a brick field, and survived until the Second World War. The buildings were damaged during the war and closed in 1944. The schools that replaced them are just as distinctive, but utterly different.

Benthal Primary and Junior Schools occupy a roughly pentagonal site bounded by Benthal Road, Ottaway Street, Rendlesham Road and Maury Road. The first school built post-war on this site was a new Infant School, opened in September 1949 by Dame Sybil Thorndike. This is a group of white buildings with flat roofs, almost all one-storey, in Modern Movement style, fronting onto Benthal Road. The school was designed by the London County Council Architect's Department under Robert Matthew and described as 'the first completed school of 11 in a new type of light construction which are being provided by the LCC to replace older schools which have been destroyed'. The classrooms, arranged on a rectilinear layout, are wonderfully light, with full-height windows. The two main classroom blocks are separated by a grassy bank and surrounded by gardens or wild grassy areas. If it were not for the looming presence of the tower blocks on nearby Nightingale Estate, you could be in the countryside!

In 1966–67 a new Infant School was built to the north of the 1949 building, which then became a junior school. The two buildings are separate, but are linked by an interconnecting corridor. Stylistically too, we enter a different era, for the eight infant classrooms are shaped like Moorish pavilions with

Benthal Primary School in 1998

curving roofs. This was the first school designed by Paul Maas of the GLC Architect's Department. Maas wrote: 'The school had to be designed in six weeks before the budget year closed … [this] didn't allow much time for research so I asked my four children what they liked and disliked about the various schools which they were attending. I also tried to recall the kinds of structures that had excited me when I was a child. The result was a classroom designed on a pinwheel plan that related to the small group style of teaching, with a form that tried to symbolize the archetypal structures of a cave and a tent (standing under the arches it recalls a cave and outside of the arches it recalls a tent). Each classroom was lit through a large central roof light, allowing a variety of standard window shapes to be positioned at children's eye levels. Each classroom had its own protected piece of nature (its courtyard) and each was scaled to the height of 5-7 year olds … I wanted Benthal to feel like a children's world in which adults were invited.' Walls link the pavilions, but arches and circular holes cut through, leading into playground. Maas described the construction: 'The arches were of on-site precast concrete, and the cavity walls had a pumice block internal skin and a hollow clay pot external skin. The external finish was a three coat cement render. The roof joists fitted into slots in the precast arches. The clerk-of-works, Mr Smith, commented that "the whole thing went together like a Meccano set". The prefabricated components and the savings on perimeter walls and volumes permitted the school to be built within the standard ministry cost allowances.' At the same time, some changes to the junior school were made, including opening up some corridors and building the water garden between the two classroom wings.

An attractive courtyard was created between the two buildings; from this the juxtaposition of the two architectural styles and attractive landscaping can best be seen. For an inner-London school, the playground is large and imaginatively planned on several levels, making the best of the unusually shaped site. The screen wall on Benthal Road has reverse-embossed lettering bearing the inscription 'Benthal Primary School' in a typically Sixties typeface. The planning of the 1967 building to complement the earlier one has been intelligently done. A blend with the 1949 building is successfully achieved by maintaining the overall low heights and the white exterior, yet each building has its own distinct architectural style. Together, they stand out from the surrounding streetscape, most of which represents the worst of post-war housing redevelopment.

Wilton Estate

Lansdowne Drive, E8

DATE   1950
ARCHITECTS   Norman & Dawbarn
CLIENT   Hackney Borough Council

Cantilevered balconies
Wilton Estate, 1998

In contrast with the monolithic style of Woodberry Down Estate which was being built at the time, this estate expresses some of the lightness of the architecture associated with the 1951 Festival of Britain. The projecting balconies, coloured facing panels and the attention to landscaping make it a classic example of the soft, Scandinavian style of the early 1950s.

Wilton Estate occupies a roughly rectangular island site bounded by Lansdowne Drive, Wilton Way, Forest Road and Greenwood Road. There are 99 flats arranged in six three-storey blocks, varying in size between two and five rooms. The layout of the blocks was adopted in order to retain existing mature trees in the middle of the site. The centre of the site is a large grassy courtyard incorporating a children's playground, laundry, workshop and pram and cycle sheds built between the trees which were retained. The central gardens are landscaped, even incorporating a grassy mound formed from spoil; this proved cheaper than removing the surplus earth. Although there is open access to the central gardens, they still retain a feeling of belonging to the flats. Each flat has its own south or west facing balcony.

Construction consists of load-bearing brick walls faced with mild stock bricks. The cantilevered balconies are of reinforced concrete cast against corrugated steel shuttering. The majority of roofs are flat, except for curved tin roofs to the tank rooms and the buildings in the courtyard. This style was also used for similar flats built later at Graham Road in an extension of the estate. The flats were originally heated by both gas and open fires.

Norman & Dawbarn were one of the leading firms of architects involved with public housing during the post-war period, and a major player in the Hackney scene.

John Scott Health Centre and Nursery School

Green Lanes, N4

DATE   1949-52
ARCHITECT   London County Council Architect's Department
              (W J Durnford and A E Miller)
CLIENT   London County Council

This Health Centre and Nursery School were planned as part of the Woodberry Down Estate (see p. 69). They stand to the south of the estate, at the junction of Green Lanes and Spring Park Drive, with superb views over the New River and reservoirs. The centre was designed by or under A E Miller of the London County Council's Hospitals and General Division in 1948, before the nationalisation of the Health Service. It is of considerable importance as 'the first [post-war health centre] in London, and the first in the whole of the country to be approved by the Minister of Health'. It was planned as one of 10 clinics to serve London, and was the only one to be purpose built. Aneurin Bevan, the Minister of Health, cut the first turf in March 1949, and the building was opened in October 1952.

The design resulted from discussions between the medical and architectural departments of the LCC and other interested parties. The aim was to provide a comprehensive range of local health authority services (GP, maternity, child welfare and school health) to about 20,000 residents from the Woodberry Down area and further afield. Facilities included GPs consulting rooms, chiropody clinic, lecture hall, dental surgery, child guidance unit, ophthalmology unit, pathological laboratory and administrative rooms. Next door is a day nursery which was planned for 42 children.

The building is two storeys high, and built of brick with fine detailing. It is roughly C-shaped, on a 1½ acre plot of land. Large windows help create an airy, light interior and capture the Fifties feel. It survives complete and largely unaltered, even down to the Crittall window frames, and in this lies much of its attractiveness.

It was first known as Woodberry Down Health Centre, but in 1965 it was renamed after Dr John Scott, a Medical Officer of Health in the LCC who died earlier that year.

John Scott Health Centre, 1998

Vaine House and Granard House

Gascoyne Estate, Hartlake Road, Hackney, E9

DATE	1955
ARCHITECT	London County Council Architect's Department (C G Weald and C St J Wilson)
CLIENT	London County Council

Granard House before refurbishment in 1998

Hackney's major homage to Le Corbusier, though the master's message is diluted here through the use of mixed development. Vaine House and Granard House are two 11-storey slab blocks each containing 105 maisonettes. This development (noted in the contemporary press as the Bentham Road scheme) was one of three London County Council estates designed by the LCC Architect's Department in the 1950s when they were experimenting with maisonette slab blocks and the narrow-frontage maisonette. This scheme was completed first, and followed by two other similar but better-known estates, Loughborough Road in Brixton and Alton West at Roehampton. All three estates show the influence of Le Corbusier's *unité d'habitation*, with tall blocks raised above a semi-open ground floor of columns, or *pilotis*, and two-storey maisonettes expressed externally in a concrete frame.

Granard House. The semi-open ground floor before refurbishment in 1998

By designing units with a width of just 12 ft. 3 in., 20% more dwellings could be fitted in and a very high population density achieved; it was said that 'this freed a high proportion of the site as open space' allowing for larger play areas in compensation. The LCC Housing Committee was concerned about adequate light penetration into the long, narrow rooms, so a prototype maisonette was built at Purley in 1952 for 'inspection and experimental purposes'. Approval of the prototype enabled the design to be used at Hackney and Roehampton. The main construction work on the Hackney site started three years later. Vaine House and Granard House form part of a large estate developed by the LCC over a long period, and eventually containing over 1,100 dwellings.

The key feature of these blocks is their concrete frames, made from components fabricated on site. This method of construction, devised in conjunction with the famous engineer F J Samuely, was relatively new. External walls are prefabricated fire-resistant wood frame panels. The two-storey units have load-bearing cross wall construction. The maisonettes are accessed from galleries running the length of the blocks on alternate floors. A central lift and staircase serves each gallery. Each maisonette has a private south-facing balcony. The overall dimensions are 17 ft. 6 in. high x 40 ft. deep x 12 ft. 3 in. wide (although the internal width measurement is just 11 ft.). Though these tall blocks represented the latest thinking of their time in planning and execution, ironically they were designed for heating by coal fires.

At the time of their completion, these blocks were regarded as setting a new standard in high–density public housing. It is worth quoting the opinion of the periodical *Prospect* in 1958: 'Until the blocks have been occupied for some time the result of the sociological experiment cannot be judged although there is no reason to doubt its success. The architectural qualities are never-the-less easily seen and extremely impressive, the relationship of unit-block-site is excellent even if somewhat overpowering in sheer mass. It is to be regretted that the demand of large scale *pilotis* and cantilevers by the architects and the complex portal frame construction by the engineer has made this building an extremely expensive experiment. The vast concrete box foundation, made necessary by the poor soil conditions could deem the whole experiment of high blocks as basically unsuitable on this site. There is little doubt however of the value of this high density development in giving a direction towards a confident urban scene … The working enthusiasm and team-work of the groups … produced what is probably the finest local government housing to be seen.'

Whatever accolades the blocks received in the architectural press of the 1950s, within forty years they were in need of drastic overhaul. In 1998 an extensive refurbishment programme was carried out including removing asbestos, improving communal areas, replacing lifts and enclosing the semi-open ground floor between the *pilotis* to house concierge facilities. Each block was given different coloured perforated metal balconies – Vaine now has blue and Granard, turquoise green. Now smartened up, the blocks have a looming presence in the landscape, like stranded liners.

The Beckers

Rectory Road, N16

DATE   1958
ARCHITECT   Frederick Gibberd with G L Downing, Borough Engineer
CLIENT   Hackney Borough Council

This estate is another example of mixed development by Gibberd, in a similar vein to the Somerford Estate, Shacklewell Road of 1946-49. The Beckers contained the 3,000th dwelling to be built in Hackney since the end of the Second World War. This milestone was marked at the opening ceremony on 19 April 1958, attended by the Mayor, Alderman B Cohen and Mrs E Beckers, who named the estate after her husband, a former councillor.

The estate consists of 148 dwellings – two blocks of three-bedroom terraced houses, one block of two-bedroom flats, and two 11-storey blocks containing bedsits and one-bedroom flats. The high-rise blocks have curved tops for the lift towers, giving the blocks a distinctive profile from a distance. The scheme also had six garages, a community hall, laundry, chapel and children's playground.

At the end of the Second World War traditional building methods continued to be favoured because the building industry was not yet ready to adopt more innovatory techniques. This situation had totally changed by the mid-1950s, when non-traditional techniques were being actively encouraged; hence the use of some taller blocks of flats on this estate, constructed of reinforced concrete. But on this estate, as elsewhere in the borough, the mixture of building heights also reflected an architectural predilection of the time. A feature of the flats was the installation of electric under-floor heating, a new concept for council flats at the time (in contrast to the solid fuel heating at Vaine House and Granard House, Hartlake Road). The floors absorb heat during the night and emit it slowly during the day. Electric fires were also provided to top up the system when required.

The Beckers, c1960

St. Michael & All Angels Church

Lansdowne Drive, London Fields, E8

DATE	1959-60
ARCHITECT	N F Cachemaille-Day
CLIENT	London Diocesan Fund

The church during construction in 1960. Looking towards the front entrance in Lansdowne Drive. Taken from Blanchard Road (now demolished)

This church was built on the west side of London Fields as a post-war replacement for a church of 1864 damaged in the Second World War which had stood on the east side of the fields. (The ruins of the church remained until c1956; the Victorian vicarage of 1873 survives.) The church, a parish hall and flat were designed by the architect N F Cachemaille-Day (1896-1976), who specialised in church buildings during a long and distinguished career. After the Second World War he was appointed Architect-Surveyor to the Archdeaconry of Hackney, and during this period he designed (or partly redesigned, following war damage) several other churches and church buildings in the area. He often worked closely with artists and craftsmen to help create works of art which complemented the building. St. Michael & All Angels is a good example of such a collaboration, where he worked with the artist John Hayward (b. 1929).

The building is 56 ft. square and rather squat-looking. The frame is reinforced concrete faced externally with brick, and the plain basic square shape is surmounted by an elegant dome of shell concrete, covered with

the architect Nugent Francis Cachemaille-Day in St. Michael & All Angels during construction in 1960

drawing of the east elevation

copper. The modest entrance porch is surmounted by an aluminium sculpture of St. Michael slaying the dragon, designed by John Hayward. Inside, the sides of the dome roof surmounting the square yield four crescent-shaped lunette windows, akin to a clerestory, containing vibrant stained glass designed by the architect; blue and yellow are used at the sides, and red above the altar showing St. Michael. The glass was made by the local Shoreditch firm of Goddard & Gibbs.

The foundation stone was laid on 7 November 1959 by the Bishop of Stepney, and the building consecrated by the Bishop of London on 11 February 1961. The new church cost £49,000, provided by the War Damage Commission, the sale of the site of the old Parish Hall, the London Diocesan Fund and the church's own appeal fund. In 1962 a magnificent set of nine murals by John Hayward were presented to the church by the Austin Abbey Memorial Trust Fund for Mural Paintings in Great Britain. They depict Old and New Testament scenes referring to the ministry of God's angels, on the side walls, and the Baptism of Christ, on the wall behind the font. They were painted on large canvases then stuck directly onto the walls, a technique known as *marouflage*. They were said to be the largest modern set of murals in the world and cost £2,880. Hayward also designed the Christus Rex (hanging cross) and the magnificent apostles' windows. Hayward worked with Cachemaille-Day on further projects, including St. Paul, West Hackney. His more recent work includes the great west window at Sherborne Abbey, completed in 1997.

The openness of the interior space is very pleasing and feels very original in design. The altar is free-standing, octagonal in shape, with a large

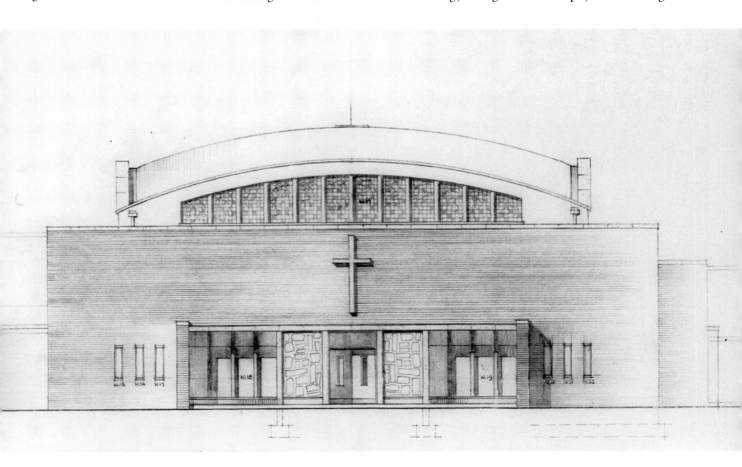

Communion rail, the whole ensemble surmounted by a 'corona on stilts'. Cachemaille-Day designed this as the centrepiece of the church, in place of an earlier design for a baldacchino which was rejected. He had used this device earlier at St. John-at-Hackney (interior renovation following fire, 1955-58) and St. Paul, West Hackney (completely rebuilt after war damage, 1958-60). Originally there was a movable glass partition behind the altar leading into the church hall; when opened up this provided extra space for worship and enabled the congregation to face the altar on three sides, but this was subsequently blocked up.

Hackney does not have many post-war churches of quality. This is a fine example for its combination of shell concrete roof and the space it creates, and the fine murals and sculpture by John Hayward, whose work is increasingly being recognised.

St. Michael & All Angels Church
in 1998

31 Kingsgate Estate

Tottenham Road, De Beauvoir, N1

DATE   1958-61
ARCHITECT   Frederick Gibberd with G L Downing, Borough Engineer
CLIENT   Hackney Borough Council

This is a later mixed development scheme resulting from Gibberd's continued association with Hackney. Three terraces of maisonettes and a block of flats are arranged around a central courtyard square. The maisonettes have two or three bedrooms, and the flats vary in size from bedsits to two bedroom flats.

The central courtyard contains a children's play area and terraces, a tenants' common room and laundry, cycle and pram stores. The ground floor maisonettes have private gardens.

The layout of the block of flats is similar to that used at The Beckers – the lift and staircase occupy the central portion, with three wings of flats attached to it. The layout is designed to give as much sound insulation as possible; two of the four flats have no party walls, whilst the other two share one. Architectural interest lies in two main design features; the terraces of maisonettes have pitched roofs running front to back, resulting in a pediment on the main elevation. This creates an interesting contrast with nearby

ingsgate Estate. Four-storey
aisonettes, 1998

housing. Arches are cut through the dividing walls at ground floor level. The second striking feature is the staircase design. The concrete casting on the underside of the staircase slopes at an angle to dizzying effect.

Mixed developments such as Kingsgate were meant to provide a variety of housing types and a visual effect of intricacy. Gibberd was a brilliant exponent of this game, not just in Hackney but around the country. What detracts from such schemes is that they destroy the pattern of the traditional street, replacing it with a pattern of blocks and spaces which relate badly to the daily pattern of people's lives. The destruction of the street is one of the main reasons why modern estates have proved so problematic and involved. Kingsgate has fared better than most in this respect.

Kingsgate Estate.
One of the staircases,
with characteristic
sloping undersides,
1998

32 Lion Boys' Club

148-152 Pitfield Street, Hoxton, N1

DATE   1961-62
ARCHITECT Francis Pollen
CLIENT   Lion Boys' Club

The Lion Boys' Club is a striking three-storey modern building at the junction of Pitfield Street and Crondall Street in Hoxton. This is an area which was badly bombed during the Second World War. The architectural practice of Francis Pollen and Philip Jebb applied for planning permission to build the club 'on derelict land' in July 1957. The gestation period for the building was fairly long, but by July 1960, a building had been designed which satisfied both client and planning authorities.

The building has three storeys and a basement. The ground floor contains a double height gym with a stage. The remainder of the first floor has a games room and coffee bar, and the second floor a play barn, roof terrace and club room. The structure is reinforced concrete with slab floors and some

he Club in 1998, before its
me was changed to Lion Club
r Young People

reinforced concrete walls. Other walls are of brick and cavity construction. The play barn is roofed with 12 in. × 12 in. glass lenses and originally had open latticed sides. The outside walls are of purple engineering brick. The main elevation has a sculpture of a lion by David John, of sheet copper.

The architect Francis Pollen (1926-87), who was in partnership with Lionel Brett (Lord Esher) during the 1960s, is little known, and few of his buildings were written up in the contemporary architectural press. He trained at Cambridge and the Architectural Association, and his early works are traditional in style. His *magnum opus* is Worth Abbey Church (1965-75). However, the Lion Boys' Club was important in his stylistic development for demonstrating his capacity to work in a modern style. It shows traits of recent architectural movements called 'The New Brutalism', particularly in the segmental concrete arches, derived from Le Corbusier.

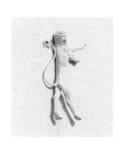

Ian Nairn in *Modern Buildings in London* (1964) wrote of the building, 'With a difficult problem, representing the quintessence of teenage touchiness, the architect has been completely sure-footed. The outside has purple brick walls, then a wavy concrete vault, then a tall covered space on the roof walled with timber slats. As cheeky and pungent as a Cockney van-driver. Inside, everything is solid (to stand up to heavy wear) but not crude; and with the variety of rooms and the way they are used it captures the need for mystery and going-the-limit which all the laudable intentions in the world cannot replace. There is a gallery from a coffee bar looking out over a stage, there are rooftop terraces; nothing is going to peel or chip. This is architecture operating at its true level to the whole range of human needs.'

33 Haggerston Girls' School

Weymouth Terrace, E2

DATE   1963-65
ARCHITECTS   Ernö Goldfinger and Hubert Bennett,
         London County Council Architect
CLIENT   London County Council

Haggerston Girls' School, 1998

Haggerston Girls' School is unusual among Hackney schools in having been designed by an internationally famous architect. The LCC normally designed its schools in-house, but in this case commissioned Ernö Goldfinger: as it turned out, this was his only secondary school project.

Goldfinger (1902-87) was born in Budapest. At the age of 17 his family moved to Vienna; a year later he visited Paris, staying there for 14 years. He studied at the Ecole des Beaux Arts where he was encouraged to employ structural rationalism based on the classical tradition. He came to believe that 'it must always be possible to see and feel how a building is supported'. He

Haggerston Girls' School.
The main circulatory space, 1998

derived much inspiration from Auguste Perret (the patron of the atelier set up by Goldfinger and others whilst they were students in Paris) and Le Corbusier. In his subsequent work the hallmarks of his style include an adherence to strictly geometric forms and a reliance on exposed concrete finishes.

The main classroom block at Haggerston School is typical of Goldfinger's style from the 1950s onwards. The concrete frame is clearly visible, and can be seen as far down as ground level; the glazed infill panels are not structural, and the same unit is repeated across the whole façade. Within this uniformity, certain ideas are emphasised, sometimes because of functional requirements within the building. The first floor projection on the front elevation houses the library and art rooms; the projection on the three upper floors of the rear elevation gives greater space in the classrooms. The partitions between classrooms are flexible, and the electricity and heating supplies are also adaptable. The vertical columns are U-shaped, doubling as vertical ducts.

The two blocks at either side of the main classroom block contrast strongly with it. Both blocks house large spaces – the school hall and the sports hall and gymnasium.

The school hall is constructed of Staffordshire Blue load-bearing bricks, and the sports hall of reinforced concrete. Goldfinger uses another distinguishing device to roof these, a deeply-coffered concrete slab. This is designed on a 2 ft. 9 in. grid, a measurement which Goldfinger traced to the dimension of the Golden Section.

The floor slabs of the main block project from the façade, supporting the glazed infill panels. In the rear projecting bay, the floor slab is extruded to form a concrete panel which frames the glazing. Treatment of the panel at the rear stair differs from the classroom panels. This difference is emphasised by the positioning of the plant room immediately above this bay.

34 Ada Street Workshops

Ada Street, E8

DATE   1965–66
ARCHITECTS   Yorke, Rosenberg & Mardall with Hubert Bennett,
            Greater London Council architect
CLIENT   Greater London Council Valuer's Department

The flatted factory in Ada Street was designed by Yorke, Rosenberg & Mardell in 1965-66 to help meet the needs of small-scale light industries in the East End. YRM began in 1944, founded by the English architect F R S Yorke, author of *The Modern House and Flat* with Frederick Gibberd; Eugene Rosenberg came from Prague; and Cyril Mardall was a Finn who had taught at the Architectural Association. Although from widely different backgrounds, they were drawn together by an underlying social concern. As their practice developed, the majority of their clients came from the public sector. They believed that 'God was in the details', and they aimed to improve the quality of public buildings rather than pushing a particular style.

As with many of YRM's buildings of this period, the façade of the Ada Street block reads as one flat plane, resembling a block of flats. The recessed areas for circulation are defined by the strong horizontal lines of the white flint-lime brick with which the building is faced. The continuous strips of windows emphasize this horizontality. They continue round the corners of the façade, a feature used in the design of YRM's own white tile-clad office building completed in 1961.

The building has a reinforced concrete frame and is eight storeys high. External cladding is of flint-lime brick, and window frames are timber, stained dark brown. There are full-length access balconies on the south elevation. The internal finishes are granolithic floors, brick walls and painted concrete ceilings. The detailing of the building is well-considered, not flimsy in any way. The building as a whole provides a substantial, robust, well-ordered solution to a building type not widely developed.

35 Christchurch Estate

Victoria Park Road, E9

DATE 1969-77
ARCHITECTS John Spence & Partners
CLIENT Crown Estate Commissioners

Victoria Park and the surrounding land were acquired by the Crown in the early 1840s, and the architect of the park, James Pennethorne, intended building spacious villas around the park. The rents from these were to offset the cost of maintaining the park. However, the villas were never quite as grand as envisaged, and the development took far longer than Pennethorne had anticipated. Thus the Crown came to own a large area of land in southern Hackney, which is one of its three principal London estates. (The other two are at Millbank and around Regents Park.) Christchurch Estate, built during the 1970s, echoes the pattern of modest Victorian terraced housing found in the neighbouring streets around Victoria Park.

Christchurch Estate, 1998

The estate is on a wedge-shaped piece of land between the Regent's Canal, Victoria Park Road and Gore Road in the south of the borough. The area was formerly occupied by Christ Church and Victorian terraced housing which had become very run-down after the Second World War. In the mid-1960s the Commissioners engaged architects John Spence & Partners to build some infill housing nearby at 89-96 Gore Road; this was followed by refurbishment of nearby Victorian properties during the 1970s. The brief for Christchurch Estate was developed by the Crown Estates Office, the letting agents, and the architects. The Commissioners wanted as wide a range of dwelling sizes as possible, and the architects were free to work within this guideline. The estate was built in three stages, starting in the east at Gore Road and gradually moving westwards. The first phase, completed in 1971, includes St. Agnes Close; the second, completed in 1974, includes Pennethorne Close, Vicars Close and The Mews, and the third, completed in 1977, includes Christchurch Square. Further housing development took place on land to the west of the estate during the 1990s.

The Crown Commissioners are neither a private developer, nor a public authority. They therefore perhaps enjoy a greater degree of freedom than other agencies when it comes to commissioning new housing. The Commissioners could be described as a paternalistic landlord, but one who looks after the estate in a model fashion. The estate provides rented housing at standards which were well above the minimum prevailing in council housing at the time. This could be achieved as the Commissioners are not subject to the cost constraints imposed on local authorities.

One of the most attractive features of Christchurch Estate is the mixture of different types of dwelling it contains. Along Victoria Park Road are four-storey high blocks with their backs to the main road. There are also mews houses for one to three people, split level over garages and partially top lit; two-storey houses for two to five people, some flats, and larger houses in the later stages of the development making a total of 149 dwellings. Construction is traditional brickwork with modern details such as aluminium sash windows in timber frames, and aluminium covered roofs. The whole development is well landscaped, using granite setts, brick retaining walls to contain grass, shrubs, old and newer trees and exotic plants. The style of the estate is modern in idiom, but the architects strove to keep it low-rise and in scale with the surrounding streets, which have predominantly Victorian housing. Cars are not banned from the estate, in fact there are 162 parking places, of which 113 are in garages. However, there is a feeling that the car is subordinate to the pedestrian, a relationship which has been well-handled by the architects.

36 Ickburgh School

Ickburgh Road, Clapton, E5

DATE **1972**
ARCHITECTS **Foster Associates**
CLIENT **Spastics Society and Prototype Unit,
with the London Borough of Hackney**

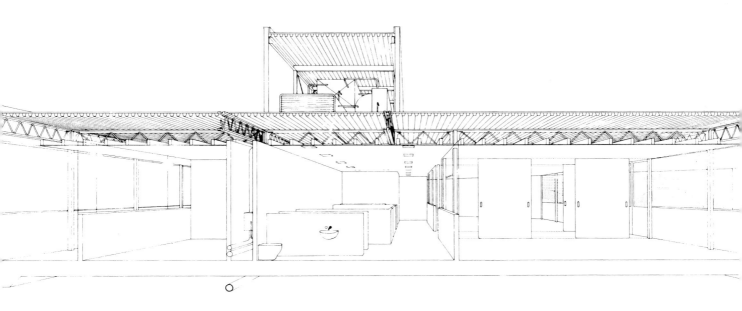

kburgh School. Sectional
rspective showing structure
d interior spaces

This building resulted from a research project undertaken by the Spastics Society. They employed Foster Associates to assess the needs and propose solutions for the 'facility needs' of the severely subnormal child. There was extensive consultation with various groups involved with the handicapped, and the architects visited several older institutions which had been used for the education of handicapped children. This led to an illustrated Design Guide which the Spastics Society published.

The next step was to build a prototype to test the proposals, and the Society approached all the London boroughs to see if a site could be donated. The Society offered to pay for the design and construction of the building. Hackney Council gave a site at the rear of an existing Junior Training School off Ickburgh Road in Clapton. Building work commenced in 1972 to Foster's designs.

The main requirement for the design was flexibility, as the education of the handicapped was under review at this time, and it was necessary to allow for possible changes. The design incorporates a central service core running across the building, forming a barrier between the public and private areas. This is surrounded by large, flexible areas with movable screens and glass partitions. Toilets and wet areas form part of the central core and are visible from the classrooms.

Structurally the building resembles an industrial shed. It has a frame of Metsec steel lattice joists supported on square tubular-steel stanchions,

Ickburgh School, 1999

bolted to a reinforced concrete raft, and covered with a steel roof deck. Walls are aluminium frames with dry linings internally, and enamelled aluminium cladding externally. The roof zone accommodates all the services and the heating system.

Ickburgh School was Foster's first non-commercial building. It is a miniature version of earlier Foster projects, but unlike most of its predecessors, its users have very specific needs. It is questionable whether this type of design, providing speed and economy of construction and maximum flexibility, is suitable for a caring building such as a school for the handicapped. It relies on the superficial application of colour – bright yellow walls, orange stanchions and carpet, pink sliding doors and inflatable play toys – to provide any real liveliness and inspiration. Once the building was in use, it was discovered that the bright colours made the children hyperactive, and the carpet had to be removed as it was absorbing too much debris. Today, it is children's work on display and other stimulating material that enlivens the building.

The building was completed in 1972 and officially opened by the Slade pop group on St. Valentine's Day, 1974.

Social housing

Church Crescent, E9

DATE   1981–84
ARCHITECTS Colquhoun & Miller
CLIENT   London Borough of Hackney

Looking north with the Church Crescent housing in the foreground and St. John of Jerusalem behind

Church Crescent curves around the Victorian church of St. John of Jerusalem with its landmark copper-clad spire by Cachemaille-Day. The houses on its south side are on awkward wedge-shaped plots. These two pairs of semi-detached villas were designed in the early 1980s as infill housing. As the surrounding urban context includes buildings ranging from the Victorian

to the modern, the architects clearly felt there was scope here for a really distinctive design.

Whilst respecting the overall height of surrounding housing, the villas are quite different from their neighbours. White rendered walls and generous overhanging eaves show Palladian influences. Built to house families of up to eight people, the villas have three storeys, with up to five bedrooms on the upper two floors. The entrance is at the side of each semi, and is dominated by a tall, narrow vertical window to the stair with small glazing panels – an instantly recognisable nod towards Mackintosh. On this elevation are two projecting bays to bedrooms at the second floor level. These bays are side lit to avoid overlooking. A projecting bay on the street elevation is full height, allowing light into the bathrooms at first floor level instead of having windows directly onto the street. At second floor level, a balcony is created to the front bedrooms. On the ground floor, the extra space created by the bay is used to give more floor space in the kitchen/dining area.

The villas are built of load-bearing concrete blocks on a brick plinth. The white finish has been created by three coats of smooth white render, reminiscent of white architecture of the 1930s. Lines were incised in the render, either harking back to the early 19th century practice of indicating fake joints to imply ashlar construction, or as a reference to panels used in 20th century construction. Window frames are of powder-coated aluminium, and the roofs have concrete slates.

The villas make an interesting contribution to this area in south Hackney, and suit the context of Church Crescent extremely well.

38 Social housing

Shrubland Road, Albion Drive and Brownlow Road, E8

DATE   1984
ARCHITECTS Colquhoun & Miller
CLIENT   London Borough of Hackney

Shrubland Road villas, 1998. Holly Street Estate can be seen in the background

This scheme is unusual in local authority housing, consisting of villas built on a series of infill sites in three neighbouring roads. The designs complement the neighbouring 19th century semi-detached, three-storey houses: the original building lines were followed and sometimes even the foundations of the earlier buildings were re-used. Materials were chosen which matched those already found in the neighbourhood – London stock bricks, reconstituted stone detailing, sash windows and slate roofs. It was also possible to retain the existing mature gardens.

However, the result is a strikingly modern interpretation, and not merely a pastiche of the originals. The houses have some classical and traditional elements, yet are at the same time modern. For example, pitched roofs were chosen, but run front to back rather than side to side. This resulted in a pedimented front, a cheaper solution than building a parapet. The accommodation ranges from one-bedroom flats to three-bedroom houses, but the façades remain the same. The basement floors are rusticated, and the entrance levels are raised.

An incongruous siting occurs where one of the houses is situated between two blocks of flats in Shrubland Road, but all the other settings are appropriate.

The houses set a precedent for local authority house building, because of the re-use of existing plots from the previous housing on the site. This is an ingenious scheme within a limited budget.

③⑨ Sutton Square

Urswick Road, E9

DATE   1983–84
ARCHITECTS   CZWG
CLIENT   Kentish Homes Ltd

Sutton Square is an interesting example of how speculative house building returned to Hackney during the 1980s boom. Much of the housing in the borough was built speculatively by the 19th century counterparts of today's builder-developers – at the height of the Victorian building boom. Typically, this meant that an architect or surveyor drew up plans (often based on those published in pattern books), whilst a builder or developer took the financial risk and had the final decision about exactly how the plans were to be executed. There was almost always a desire or pressure to cut costs during the building process, but the system was successful in housing a vastly expanded middle class population. In Hackney, this kind of arrangement had almost ceased following the Second World War, as most post-war building activity took place in the public sector. The post-war middle classes largely bought Georgian or Victorian properties, and contributed to the gentrification of many areas. But what if they wanted to buy new homes?

In the 1980s boom Hackney became popular again as a place with affordable housing near to the City and West End. A young architectural practice, Campbell Zogolovitch Wilkinson & Gough, became involved in designing several speculative houses and developments in Hackney, Camden and elsewhere. Their first scheme in Hackney was for 14 houses at Harrowgate Road near Victoria Park, completed in 1983. These are three-storey houses in pairs or fours, in an ordinary street of Victorian terraced houses; brick-built with pitched roofs, an integral garage, and stuccoed frontispieces painted pink. In the background loom the newly-refurbished Corbusian blocks of Vaine House and Granard House on the Gascoyne Estate, a stark juxtaposition of the modern with the post-modern.

Sutton Square is a much more substantial development. It is in the centre of Hackney on the site of the former Metal Box factory, adjacent to the Tudor building of Sutton House, the Georgian buildings of Sutton Place, and St. John-at-Hackney with its spacious and leafy churchyard. It is unashamedly not what it purports to be – a Georgian London square. Rather, this is a Georgian-style development of 52 houses and a small block of flats with some references to the classical style, and dollops of post-modern stucco and colour. The similarity with the Victorian speculative developers of 19th century Hackney is that CZWG produced private house designs for use under licence by the developers Kentish Homes. For about £250 per unit, standard drawings, layouts and elevations were provided, and the fee paid after planning permission was given. That more or less ended the architects' involvement with the scheme. Kentish Homes built and supervised the development, broadly following the plans, but with the option to amend them if required. Kentish Homes had exclusivity on the designs in Hackney and Tower Hamlets, but CZWG were free to market them elsewhere. Sutton Square is a narrow, oblong square with long terraces of two and three-storey houses on three sides. The central area is given over to a garden and car parking. A pair of loggias mark the entrance to the square from Urswick Road.

For many people who seek (and can afford) modern housing in a pleasant location, this has proved a very successful place to live. Its post-modern touches now seem less outrageous than when it was first built, and the main criticism to be levelled at it is that it feels so obviously like a private enclave, turning its back on the surrounding area.

Sutton Square, 1999

④ Homerton Hospital and Education Centre

Homerton Grove, E9

DATE   1980–87
ARCHITECTS   YRM Architects & Planners
CLIENT   City and Hackney Health Authority

Homerton Hospital, 1998

Homerton Hospital was built in the early 1980s. It replaced two Victorian institutional buildings on the same site: the Eastern Fever Hospital which opened in 1871, one of the first three foundations of the Metropolitan Asylums Board to treat fever and smallpox, and the City of London Union Workhouse. The two institutions were amalgamated in 1921, and although major rebuilding was planned as early as 1939, this did not take place until the 1980s. By then the buildings had become very run-down, and it was high time for a new hospital building.

The new hospital has 444 beds in four linked two-storey pavilions. There is also a separate two-storey Education Centre. The low-rise design of the main buildings gives the hospital a friendly feel. The major design feature is the use of pitched roofs. These provide generous space for the mechanical services which can easily be taken down to wards and operating theatres below. Easy access to services was a prime consideration in hospital design at this time, an idea promoted by Ministry of Health architects. The buildings have reinforced concrete frames, clad with yellow bricks, chosen to harmonise with the predominant use of London stock bricks in the surrounding streets. Roofs have deep eaves and blue-black slate. Although car parks predominate at the front of the site, the landscaping around the buildings, with pergolas, window boxes and well thought-out planting make this a very pleasant environment. The pergolas incorporate Victorian cast iron columns recycled from the covered walkways at the old Eastern Fever Hospital site. Looking out from the hospital there are many views into the landscaped courts and gardens. Paths through these gardens have become popular pedestrian routes through the hospital complex.

The building has a coherence, yet there is scope for flexibility and planned growth in the future.

41 Schonfeld Square

Lordship Road, Stoke Newington, N16

DATE	1991–94
ARCHITECTS	Hunt Thompson Associates
CLIENT	Agudas Israel Housing Association

This highly unusual housing association development has been built to serve the Orthodox Jewish community who have made this part of Hackney their home. It is named after Dr Avigdor Schonfeld who came from Hungary to lead the community and became the rabbi of the most flourishing synagogue in the area.

The site was previously occupied by Bearsted Hospital, another Jewish institution, which was demolished in the 1970s. A deep rectangle of land was available for the new development, stretching west from Lordship Road, and it was decided to arrange the housing around a square at the end of a turning off the road. Crudely speaking, the layout is a cul-de-sac but it has none of the banal, road-dominated characteristics of the normal cul-de-sac. This is definitely a square at the heart of a distinctive community.

The entrance to the development is marked by two four-storey buildings, one circular and one square, both topped by cupolas. These provide housing for the elderly and the disabled. In the street towards the square and in the square itself, there are houses and flats in three storey blocks and terraces. These include a wide range of accommodation from one-bedroom flats to five-bedroom houses. Everything is in brick with slate roofs and deep eaves. As well as their cupola lanterns, the entrance blocks have two nice decorative touches typical of the post-modern mood of the early 1990s: banded glazed brickwork in their attic storeys, and fat sturdy columns supporting the broad lintels in their entrances. The equally interesting circular towers, housing spiral cantilevered staircases, are hidden from view behind the blocks.

Apart from its layout and architectural quality, what distinguishes Schonfeld Square are the special features designed for the observance of orthodox Jewish ceremonies. There are kosher kitchens with separate areas for cooking milk- and meat-based dishes, and in the sheltered accommodation for the elderly, there is a Passover kitchen. Also, throughout the housing there are succohs – rooms with removable roofs where the men folk can eat under the stars during the autumn festival of succoh. There cannot be many other housing association projects which have had to meet such exacting requirements, but the fact that they have been successfully incorporated in this design shows what can be achieved by involving those who are going to live in the new housing.

42 Garden gazebo

Albion Square, E8

DATE 1995
ARCHITECT David French
CLIENTS David French and Fiona and Sandy MacLennan

emi-detached gazebo straddling two
Albion Square gardens

This Gothic-style gazebo, or summer house, is a beautiful structure, and also a most unusual solution to a problem. Two neighbours had considered erecting sheds in their neighbouring gardens in Albion Square, and this led to the idea of building a shared gazebo which straddles both gardens. It was designed by David French. It is octagonal, with two sets of interconnecting doors on the dividing line between the two gardens. These can be left open in times of cordial relations, or closed when privacy is desired. A small portion of the original garden wall, dating from when the houses were built in the 1840s, was demolished to make way for the gazebo.

The gazebo is made of timber, with gothic windows and a lead-covered roof. It was made by Reg Hardington, an expert joiner, and pre-assembled before erection on site. The ground level differed between the two gardens, so it had to be raised on one side before building commenced. The gardens are each about 22 metres long and 8 metres wide, and the gazebo occupies about 3 square metres in each garden.

This ingenious little building is testimony that with the right effort and imagination, architectural quality can be achieved even in the smallest and most unusual location.

43 Wick Village

Hackney Wick, E9

DATE 1993-95
ARCHITECTS Levitt Bernstein Associates
CLIENT London Borough of Hackney

Wick Village forms part of the comprehensive redevelopment of the Trowbridge Estate at Hackney Wick. Densely packed Victorian terraces of the mid- to late-19th century were the first houses on this site, but by the 1960s they had been earmarked for slum clearance. In their place, the Trowbridge Estate was built for the Greater London Council in 1967-70. It contained seven 21-storey system-built tower blocks and 285 low-rise houses – a total of approximately 850 dwellings. It was one of five major estates in the borough built during the late 1960s and 1970s which have been scheduled for comprehensive redevelopment. (The other four are Holly Street, Nightingale, New Kingshold and Clapton Park.) Several of these estates were completed as the enquiry into the Ronan Point disaster of 1968 was proceeding, so many remained empty until 1974 when the report on safety was issued.

Hackney Wick lies in the easternmost part of the borough, and is bounded by Eastway, the Hackney Cut Navigation and Hackney Marshes. The surrounding layout of roads, motorways, railways and canal means that the area is almost cut off. By the 1980s, several factors had led to the area becoming very depressed: the combination of large scale demolition of the original Victorian housing; the loss of community associated with it; the poor quality of the Sixties housing which replaced it; and a decline in employment traditionally available in the docks and elsewhere in the East End. The tower blocks had become extremely run down and unpopular with residents. Flats in these blocks were particularly unsuitable for families.

In 1982 control of the estate passed to the London Borough of Hackney, followed by proposals by the GLC to demolish and redevelop the estate. Three of the seven high-rise blocks were demolished in 1986. Attempts to demolish the first block made the national headlines when it failed to collapse as planned. But the programme went no further. By the early 1990s the tenants in the four remaining tower blocks had become desperate for an improvement in their living conditions. A scheme to redevelop the remaining blocks and the rest of the estate was encouraged by the council. Supported by Tenant Action, the high-rise tenants formed a co-operative in 1991, persuading the council to work with them. The co-operative became and remained involved in appointing consultants to carry out redevelopment work and considering the future management of the estate.

It was not economically viable to refurbish the tower blocks. Those tenants were offered new housing which was to be built on the site of the three blocks already demolished; this became Wick Village. They were able to participate fully in the commissioning and design of the new (low-rise) housing. This process of negotiation enabled the tenants to make real choices about their future homes so that they could identify with the place where they were to live.

123 new dwellings replaced the tower blocks. These are traditionally built houses and flats arranged around two courtyards, encouraging a feeling of community and security. The best has been made of existing features in the landscape, such as the canal, which now has attractive terraced housing alongside. Key elements include traditional family housing, good quality landscaping, well-planned road layouts and play areas. London stock and red brick has been used, with traditional pitched roofs with generous overhangs. Oriel windows and entry porches are distinctive architectural elements of the scheme. Tenants were given the opportunity to personalise their homes in several ways, with a choice of internal layouts, finishes, fixtures, colours, planting, fencing and so on. This encouraged a sense of ownership. Parking spaces have been included at a ratio of 1:1.

Wick Village was built between 1993 and 1995 and the four remaining tower blocks were subsequently demolished in 1995 and 1996. The village is now managed by a Tenant Management Co-operative, the first such formed in the borough. As far as the rest of the estate goes, the 1960s low-rise housing was retained at the request of residents, and has been refurbished to the same standard as the new housing. The whole estate now contains 505 dwellings.

Although this major redevelopment was subject to stringent financial arrangements made between a (then) very left-wing council and a (then) very right-wing government, the scheme benefited from the financial climate of the early 1990s when a scarcity of work in the construction industry resulted in good value for money. Both building and landscaping are of very high quality. The combination of several ingredients – the residents' drive and aspirations, architects' experience of similar schemes, sufficient planning time and training for the residents to enable them to make informed decisions – has resulted in a development where a sense of community has been recreated. Wick Village is maturing well and is cherished by those who live there.

ick Village. Housing by
e Hackney Cut Navigation

44 Rushton Street Surgeries

Hoxton, N1

DATE 1995-96
ARCHITECTS Penoyre & Prasad
CLIENT East London and the City Health Authority

These doctors' surgeries were built as a result of a survey conducted in the late 1980s which revealed that South Hoxton had a large number of small GP practices in unsuitable premises. The health authority felt it desirable to bring together several of these practices under one roof, and sought a suitable site in the area. The Family Practitioner Committee acted as facilitator, bringing together four separate GP practices who didn't previously know each other in a 'shotgun marriage'. A local firm of architects was engaged, with the brief that the building should be flexible enough to allow for future developments in general practice. The design resulted from lengthy consultations with the doctors. (The surgeries are an example of an early 'private finance initiative' scheme, whereby they were built by a developer, owned by an investor, leased by the health authority and sub-leased to the four medical practices.)

The result is a striking blue and white three storey building situated south of Shoreditch Park, facing north west. It was designed to have a civic presence as it is visible from all around. The form of the building was partly dictated by a requirement for off-street car parking on a fairly tight site. The ground floor divides into four zones of use: firstly, car parking and entrances; secondly, administration, records and reception; thirdly, public areas – reception and waiting areas; and fourthly clinical rooms for consulting and treatment. The first floor steps out over the parking bays, sheltering the entrance to the building. The consulting rooms on this floor have attractive bay windows (offering views over the park) which contain wash-basins. This is reflected in the ripple effect of the external wall, which is white with timber fins, a design inspired by Aalto. There are also further multi-purpose rooms on this floor. Tall, slender columns support the second floor, which contains flexible office space suitable for use by community groups or classes and a separate caretaker's flat.

The building has a steel frame infilled with concrete blocks, and precast floors. There is a skin of external insulation and render. This is a highly-insulated structure to keep energy running costs to a minimum. The roof is of deep profiled aluminium, and is shaped, rising up on the left-hand side. The architects have used colour in a striking way: the front façade is mediterranean blue (a colour they have often favoured), interrupted by the white ripple wall with timber struts at surgery level, the whole effect topped by the overhang of the sweeping roof. Internal partitions between surgeries can be easily removed in the future, allowing for a different configuration of rooms or changes in general practice.

Rushton Street Surgeries brings a dash of life and colour to the otherwise bleak area of Shoreditch Park. It is a strong enough design to hold its own in unpromising surroundings, yet sensitive enough to be welcoming to those who visit it.

Rushton Street Surgeries, 1999

Hackney Community College, Shoreditch Campus

Falkirk Street, Hoxton, N1

DATE	1992–97; Art, Media and Design Centre 1998–99
ARCHITECTS	Hampshire County Architects and Perkins Ogden Architects
CLIENT	Hackney Community College

Hackney Community College is a further education campus built to consolidate several facilities from across the borough and unite them on a single site. The new campus is in the south of the borough, on a roughly rectangular plot bounded by Falkirk Street, Hoxton Street and a line west of Kingsland Road. The area was formerly occupied by densely populated Victorian terraces and some schools. Complications of land ownership meant that the college could not purchase all the properties on the plot, so odd pockets of shops, businesses and pubs remain on the perimeter of the site, breaking up the street façades of the college. Although the area may be described as economically deprived, Hoxton is now enjoying a period of regeneration and even trendiness.

The entrance to the college in Falkirk Street is marked by two tall towers. Only glimpses of the campus can be had from the surrounding streets, but once inside, the whole becomes easier to understand. The buildings are

Hackney Community College. The northern inner courtyard, with amphitheatre leading to the library and learning resource centre

arranged round two formal courtyards. The northern courtyard has a sunken stone amphitheatre leading to the library and learning resource centre in the semi-basement. In the southern courtyard, mature plane trees have been retained, complemented by lawns and interesting planting. Two former LCC Edwardian board schools on the site have been retained and refurbished as part of the campus. The new teaching facilities are mostly in three storey blocks of attractive pale stock brick, but laid in a rather uninteresting bond. These blocks have been designed to be flexible and adaptable for future use. Simple sun canopies of timber, steel and fabric add interest to the buildings, old and new.

The only building to front Kingsland Road is the Arts, Media and Design Centre to the south east of the site, opened in 1999. Taller than other buildings on the campus, this functions as a landmark on this main road, with a three storey glass atrium and circular staircase tower. A Sports Centre is under construction at the north east of the campus.

The longest frontage of the college is on Hoxton Street, where the development includes a new Public Library. The long brick wall onto the street is punctuated by triangular window bays and by sturdy wrought iron gates designed by Matthew Fedden. The gates allow views into the two internal courtyards, and of specially commissioned pieces of sculpture.

This is a well-designed facility, with a very pleasant environment inside. It is a shame that the public are excluded from using the courtyards which are among the most pleasant public spaces in this part of the borough.

46 Lux Building

Hoxton Square, N1

DATE   1997
ARCHITECTS Maccreanor Lavington
CLIENT   Glasshouse Investments

opposite Lux Building, 1999

The striking new Lux Building in Hoxton Square houses several art and media facilities including a gallery for new media and electronic art, a cinema, café bar, studios and offices. Hoxton Square was laid out in the 17th century, but by the mid-19th century most of the Georgian houses were in workshop use, many in the furniture trade. Today the square is home to a variety of buildings – church, school, warehouses, workshops, housing and a café. The Lux Building replaces some derelict timber yards on the west side of the square.

The architect's original brief was for a shell and core building, but prospective media tenants became involved at an early stage; London Electronic Arts and the London Film Makers Co-operative. Their requirements influenced the design.

The building splits into two unequal halves, reflecting the original plot layout. The left hand part is four bays wide and six storeys high; the right hand part three bays wide and five storeys high. A lift and staircase are situated in the middle of the building. The structure is a reinforced concrete frame. The front and rear façades have precast concrete beam and concrete elements clad externally in brick. Blue-grey engineering bricks used for the cladding were chosen for their evenness of colour, and give an industrial, monolithic feel to the building. Despite this, the brick is not structural, rather the piers act as framing for the deep-set windows. The effect of the main façade is of a relentlessly regular grid. There are no concessions to conservation here. To counter the deep site and allow as much light as possible into the building, the roof is fully glazed and almost all the windows are full height.

The ground floor houses an art cinema and the Blue Note Café, the latter a typical late 1990s concrete experience. On the first floor is the gallery for new media and electronic art. This has screens at the windows which can be used for projections from the square. The remainder of the building is divided between teaching space, editing suites, studios and offices.

The distinctiveness of this building is justified by its public role. It remains to be seen whether it will mature as pleasantly as its more traditionally designed neighbours.

47 The Geffrye Museum Extension

Kingsland Road, E2

DATE   1996–98
ARCHITECTS   Branson Coates (with Sheppard Robson)
CLIENT   The Trustees of The Geffrye Museum

The Geffrye Museum, easily one of the most delightful museums in London, started life in 1714 as a set of almshouses built by the Ironmongers Company. In the early 20th century, when the Ironmongers decided that Shoreditch was too insalubrious an area for the old people in their care, the London County Council stepped in and bought the buildings. The gardens were

opened to the public and the almshouses were converted in 1912-13 to a museum of woodwork and furniture, reflecting some of the trades found locally. Nowadays the exhibits are organised as a series of recreated interiors, from the 16th century to the present day, which fill the main range of the almshouse building on either side of the chapel.

The new extension, opened at Christmas 1998, is a brilliant solution to the two main problems that the museum has experienced. First, it provides space for more displays and better facilities for school parties and the public. Secondly, it does this in a horseshoe-shaped block which helps solve the circulation problem of a building which is essentially one long corridor. People are now gently turned around by following the curved layout and so come back into the main building after visiting the extension. The new room displays are on the same levels as the old ones; below them, reached by a spiral staircase, are offices, a special exhibition area and rooms for use by schools. The new block has been built on a small playground at the south-east corner of the almshouses and can barely be seen from the forecourt garden, thereby maintaining the integrity of the original frontage.

The design by Branson Coates (with Alan Baxter and Associates, Engineers) is an ingenious combination of different forms of construction. From the outside what is most striking is the brickwork of the horseshoe, laid not in level courses, but in spirals like twisted geological strata. Above the walls can be seen the slate roof over the main display areas. Going inside, the chief surprise is the steel diagrid roof clad in copper which covers the hollow in the horseshoe and flows outwards to connect the extension with the existing building. Then finally there is the staircase which leads down to the lower floor – an exciting reinforced concrete spiral which seems to float between the two levels. The extension forms an ideal complement to the 18th century building, but is unmistakably a 1990s design.

The Geffrye Museum extension: an aerial view taken during construction in 1998. The 18th century almshouses and garden are in the top right of the photo

48 Private housing

1 Truman's Road, Shacklewell, N16

DATE · 1988-98
ARCHITECTS AND CLIENTS · Dominic and Henrietta Cullinan and Ivan and Roxanne Harbour

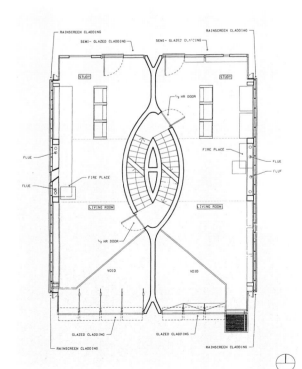

1 Truman's Road. Plan of first floor showing the double helix staircase layout, 1997

This building is a pair of semi-detached houses designed and built by two architects, Dominic Cullinan and Ivan Harbour, for their families. They met whilst searching for a plot on which to self-build and joined forces to realise the project. They searched for about three years before purchasing this plot in 1988. It had originally been a car park at the back of a former cinema on Stoke Newington Road, and had then been used as a car lot in the 1980s. The previous owner of the plot had unsuccessfully tried to obtain planning permission for six flats. Cullinan and Harbour originally envisaged two detached houses, but on this particular site, which is deep and narrow, it was difficult to incorporate the statutory gap between houses required by planning regulations. Eventually they decided to build a pair of semi-detached houses, and planning permission was granted in 1989.

The planners wanted the building to look much more traditional, and they also wanted drawings done 'properly' with a ruler! These slight hitches were eventually overcome, and the result is a strikingly modern building, incorporating many different materials, in particular concrete, anodised aluminium and timber. Most self-build projects use traditional materials, but Cullinan and Harbour opted for an in-situ reinforced concrete structure, for which they designed and built the shuttering. The surface finish of the concrete is left exposed internally, for its visual effect and also perhaps as a reminder of the heroic episodes involved in getting the whole thing built.

The building is three storeys, topped with two differently designed small cabins of timber and glass. There are excellent views from the rooftop, especially to the city in the south. Builders were engaged to lay the ground floor slab, under-floor services and some of the foundations, but otherwise Cullinan and Harbour have done all the construction work themselves with the help of family and friends. As the site is deep and narrow, the houses overhang the pavement at the front (facing north) by c1.2 metres, yielding extra room space from the first floor upwards. The architects were concerned that a traditional staircase arrangement would reduce the overall room space, so they designed an ingenious curving staircase in the form of a double helix. This can best be described as two strands of a plait which intertwine, with each staircase entirely self-contained. The staircases are cantilevered, and are made of reinforced concrete, with each step precast on the ground. Should the houses ever be sold, it would be a real challenge for an estate agent to describe this highly original arrangement, not just because of the interlocking stairs, but also because the floor plan changes from floor to floor.

The walls of the houses are 200mm thick. At each level, the central section of the floor is concrete with underfloor heating, while the rest of the floor has conventional timber joists. The south face is entirely glazed, with 6 metre high aluminium mullions imported from France. The east and west walls are clad with E-flex cladding, a material which is water-resistant and akin to 'eternit' artificial slates.

Both Cullinan and Harbour had been working on large-scale fast-track projects whilst designing and building their own houses – quite a contrast in time-scales, as this building has taken 10 years of weekends to complete. It is a fascinating addition to the Shacklewell streetscape, particularly as the surrounding area contains unremittingly dull and poor quality public housing. Hackney would gain immensely if other leftover sites were used in an equally imaginative way.

Truman's Road, 1998

49 Social housing

Murray Grove, Hoxton, N1

DATE   1998–99
ARCHITECTS Cartwright Pickard
CLIENT   Peabody Trust

The Peabody Trust (founded in 1862) is the largest housing association in London, and is therefore one of the major providers of social housing for rent in the capital. Its many new building projects mean that it plays a considerable role in economic and social regeneration.

This development of apartments for rent in Murray Grove/Shepherdess Walk is one of several sites currently being developed by the Trust in Hackney. Despite its proximity to the City, the area has suffered from a post-war decline in industry, and redevelopment of variable quality during the same period. What is particularly interesting about the project is that it represents a revival of large-scale prefabrication in housing. A combination of high land prices in south east England, and a shortage of skilled labour, has put the cost of traditional house building beyond the reach of many social housing providers. The Peabody Trust was also concerned to take steps to meet the predicted increase in demand for housing by exploring faster methods of construction. This scheme was therefore a prototype, with funding provided by Peabody and English Partnerships, and land – a brownfield site last used as a car park – provided by the London Borough of Hackney.

The Murray Grove development comprises 30 one- and two-bedroom flats for rent by single young people, couples and flat sharers who cannot afford a mortgage, but who do not qualify for social housing. The flats are made from modules designed and manufactured off-site by Yorkon, a subsidiary of Portakabin. Modules consist of panels which are a sandwich of rigid steel, insulation and plasterboard, ceiling or floorboards. Each module measures 3 metres high × 3.2 metres wide x 8 metres deep and comes fully equipped with plumbing, electrics, doors, windows, bathroom and kitchen fittings, tiles and carpets. The completed modules were transported from the factory in York and delivered to the site by articulated lorry, then winched into place. All this is a far cry from typical prefabs of the post-war period where generally just separate components were manufactured off-site.

The layout consists of two rows of flats at right angles linked by a central tower at the corner. The units on Shepherdess Walk were craned into place over five days from 29 March to 2 April 1999, and the Murray Grove row in mid-April. The project was on-site for just six months, and completed in September 1999. The blocks are five storeys high with deck access at the rear. Lightweight steel balconies and access decks echo the modular construction of the units. There is terracotta tile cladding on the front elevations and timber on the back. The central tower of glass contains the lift and stairs. The inner courtyard contains just three car parking spaces and a bicycle shed, in keeping with Peabody's desire to encourage sustainable developments; the

Murray Grove apartments.
module being winched into place
n Shepherdess Walk, April 1999

site is near to central London and public transport is plentiful in this area. The flats are designed to be both highly energy-efficient and low-maintenance.

The development is innovative in its use of new techniques, and also offered economies of time in construction. If successful, the method may be used more widely by the Peabody Trust and other developers in the UK. In keeping with the ground-breaking nature of the project, a website showed progress throughout the construction process, including photographs updated hourly provided by on-site cameras.

⓼ **Clissold Sports Centre**

Clissold Road, Stoke Newington, N16

DATE	1998–
ARCHITECTS	Hodder Associates
CLIENT	London Borough of Hackney

Clissold Sports Centre promises to be one of the most exciting buildings built in Hackney in recent years. It follows a distinguished line of designs for swimming pools in the borough, beginning with Hackney Baths (now the King's Hall Leisure Centre) of 1896-97 by Harnor & Pinches, Haggerston Public Baths of 1904 by Alfred Cross and the London Fields Lido of 1932. Clissold replaces an earlier baths by Hobden & Porri of 1930 on the same site.

The form of the building is not surprisingly almost dictated by its contents. It is effectively a building within a box – an internal cruciform shape divides the space into four main areas. The external box results from non-structural cladding around it. Two of the four main areas contain swimming pools (a main pool 25 × 17 metres, and a training pool 25 × 13 metres), the third is a sports hall and the fourth is the entrance concourse with café-bar, creche, office, lift and stairs. The cruciform itself has a concrete frame, and contains changing facilities, a children's play area, etc. The entrance to the complex is at the north east corner of the building, where a covered courtyard paved with silver grey tiles leads into the building.

Stylistically, one of the most interesting and complex features of the building is the challenging roof design by Hodder Associates and engineers Whitby & Bird. This splits into two symmetrical halves divided by a central spine wall (one axis of the cruciform) running north–south. The roof is supported off the spine wall, and on the east and west sides by six Y-shaped steel columns which stand in front of the wall line. The roof design features twenty 'toroid' or shell-shaped segments rising out of a flat plane (torus = ring shaped with a circular cross-section). Each toroid might be described as akin to an orange segment, therefore yielding two long sides which can be glazed. Thus the roof contains a series of forty clerestory windows – the architect's inspired solution to allowing as much light into the building as possible. The roof structure was made from steel in Wetherby, Yorkshire, much of it prefabricated for assembly on site. The use of bifurcating columns may be influenced by the roof structure at Foster Associates' Stansted Airport terminal (1986), but its origin really lies in Tobacco Dock, Wapping of 1811-14 where the (cast iron) columns supporting the roof split into four branches rather than two, resembling trees. The architect used a similar structure to support an over-arching roof at his Colne Swimming Pool, Lancashire (1992). The cladding is glass around the pools, whilst terracotta bricks (made in France) form rainscreen cladding on the north, south and west elevations.

When first announced, the Clissold project was described as 'an attempt to synthesise a sustainable sports centre, and one which has an urban responsiveness acting as a catalyst for localised regeneration'. Put simply, this means it will be an excellent sports facility for the northern part of the borough. When completed, its distinctive, modern design will mark a new maturity in the high tech architecture of Hackney.

posite Clissold Sports Centre. he steel roof structure being ected, April 1999

lodel of Clissold Sports Centre, ith a bird's eye view of the steel d glass roof structure.

Index

Sources of illustrations

The author and publishers are grateful to copyright holders for permission to reproduce material listed below. (Numbers refer to pages.)

Alan Baxter and Associates 99, 110
British Architectural Library, RIBA, London 79
The Conway Library, Courtauld Institute of Art 27, 32, 59, 63, 72, 73, 74, 75, 76, 80, 81, 82, 83, 85, 86, 87, 89, 95, 97, 98, 105, 109
Cullinan Harbour Architects 112
English Heritage & National Monuments Record 24, 29, 30, 35, 36, 49, 51, 52, 53, 60, 61
Foster and Partners 91
Hackney Archives 17, 25, 26, 33, 40, 47, 54, 55, 62, 67, 69, 77
Bill Hall 78, 79
Hodder Associates (© Putler/Armiger) 117
Kida Katsuhisa 113
London Metropolitan Archives 21, 22, 23, 42-43, 45, 46
Paul Maas 71
Marianne Majerus 101
Peabody Trust 115
Peter Davies Photography 116
Simpson Archive FRONT COVER, 1, 37, 38, 39